PUBLIC INTELLECTUALISM
AND
SOCIOPOLITICAL INQUIRY
THROUGH METAPHOR AND MUSING

VOLUME 2

I0553176

Kenneth K. Mwenda
PhD, LLD, DSc(Econ)

GIFT *Certificate*

TO:

_____

_____

_____

FROM:

_____

_____

DATE: _____

Would you like to buy a copy of
**PUBLIC INTELLECTUALISM AND SOCIOPOLITICAL INQUIRY
THROUGH METAPHOR AND MUSING?**

Please visit:
http://www.kennethmwenda.com/books

PUBLIC INTELLECTUALISM
AND
SOCIOPOLITICAL INQUIRY
THROUGH METAPHOR AND MUSING

VOLUME 2

Kenneth K. Mwenda
PhD, LLD, DSc(Econ)

www.africa**in**canadapress.com

TORONTO, CANADA – 2016

Public Intellectualism and Sociopolitical Inquiry Through Metaphor and Musing

PUBLISHED BY:

AFRICA IN CANADA PRESS

18A-100 Westmore Drive, Toronto, ON   M9V 5C3, CANADA
Tel: 1 (416) 644-1106,   Fax: 1 (416) 644-1126
http://www.africaincanadapress.com

AFRICA IN CANADA PRESS is committed to publishing works by authors of African descent in Canada and abroad with excellence.

COVER DESIGN & TYPESETTING BY:

www.diamondbooks.ca

PAPERBACK EDITION -V2 : ISBN: 978-1-988357-19-5 – AFRICA IN CANADA PRESS
E-BOOK -V2:   ISBN: "   "   "   – DIAMOND PUBLISHERS

PRINTED IN CANADA

INTERNATIONAL ACCLAIM

for

PUBLIC INTELLECTUALISM
AND
SOCIOPOLITICAL INQUIRY
THROUGH METAPHOR AND MUSING

"Certainly one of the top twenty-five (25) intellectuals from Africa to grace the world stage in the last two decades, Professor Mwenda's richness of thought is displayed in the depth and breadth of his trend-setting intellectual contributions (ICs). His ICs have largely, but not exclusively, been in the field of contemporary and comparative Law and Africa's development. The current book, however, is a refreshing reminder that intellectual heavyweights do, in fact, have a lighter side!"

- **Prof. Gerry Nkombo Muuka, PhD**
Associate Dean and Coordinator of
Graduate Programs

Arthur J. Bauernfeind College of Business
Murray State University, Kentucky, USA.

"Professor Mwenda is back again with yet another brilliant piece of work. In this book, he provides thought provoking explorations of socio-political themes using axioms, adages and proverbs. The result is an educational and entertaining piece of work that will appeal to readers from all walks of life – the academics, intellectually inclined as well as the casual reader. This book has something for everyone. It resonates well in all cultural settings and quite frankly it is hard to put the book down once one starts reading it. It is certainly a must read."

- **Charles Leyeka Lufumpa, PhD**
Director, Statistics Department

African Development Bank Group
Abidjan, Cote D'Ivoire

"Prof. Kenneth Kaoma Mwenda is a renowned thought leader on legal and financial matters. His extensive writings have so far targeted the 'learned minds'. In his latest book, 'Public Intellectualism and Socio-political Inquiry through Metaphor and Musing', he is in an amazing innovation addressing both the initiated as well as the uninitiated. It is an approach all intellectuals should attempt to do if they are to remain relevant to their societies."

- **Caleb M. Fundanga, PhD**
Former Governor, Bank of Zambia

President, Institute for Finance and Economics (Zambia), **Harare, Zimbabwe.**

"A timely, valuable and insightful contribution to contemporary socio-legal and political thought at a critical juncture in public intellectualism, rightly at the frontiers of thought leadership and social action."

-    **H.E. Robinson Kaleb Zulu**
Chairperson, Meanwood Group of Companies

Honorary Consul of the Republic of Korea to Zambia
Lusaka, Zambia & Leeds, United Kingdom.

"A very engaging book; reflecting Africa's new mindset towards posterity and resonates well with the growing passion for knowledge and personal development across the globe."

-   **Chibamba Kanyama**
Former Director-General, Zambia National
Broadcasting Corporation (ZNBC)

Currently with the Bretton Woods Institutions
Washington DC, USA.

"An eclectic and very thought-provoking collection of original perspectives. This book truly reflects Professor Mwenda's global character and intellectual quality. Well worth the read."

-      **Kelvin Arthur Dalrymple**
Senior Advisor to the Executive Director
for Canada, Ireland and the Caribbean

International Monetary Fund (IMF)
Washington DC, USA.

DEDICATION

St Jude;

Pray for Us.

ACKNOWLEDGEMENT

To my many students and former students worldwide at the various international universities where I have taught, thank you for being promising leaders for the next generation. That a number of my former law students have gone on to become notable Supreme Court judges, Constitutional Court judges, Court of Appeal judges and High Court judges, including an eminent Chief Justice, while others continue to serve as law professors, diplomats and ambassadors, as well as judicial clerks and prominent Cabinet Ministers, is only the beginning of the story. For, there are also those that have held or continue to hold senior positions at the World Bank, the African Development Bank, the Common Market for Eastern and Southern Africa, and many other international organizations. I am truly humbled and grateful to God, Jehovah, Almighty, for all these blessings.

Special thanks also go out to all friends and colleagues (as well as my family members, including my wife and son) who provided comments on the various sayings, musings and metaphors in this book. Their tireless contributions helped to sharpen my views on a number of issues. My other thanks go out to **Africa in Canada Press** for the timely and efficient publication of the book. **Diamond Books - Canada** is also hereby acknowledged for the excellent typesetting work and the preparation of the cover design.

TABLE OF CONTENTS

- *Kenneth K. Mwenda*

FOREWORD

While Richard Posner writes that the craft of public intellectualism is declining, Prof. Kenneth K. Mwenda's is on the rise. In March 2001, Zambia's leading private newspaper, The Post, headlined a commendation letter written by a prominent Zambian Journalist, Chibamba Kanyama, on a then budding young African legal scholar, Kenneth Mwenda. The author of that commendation letter, Chibamba Kanyama, now serving as Advisor in the Communications Department of the International Monetary Fund (IMF) in Washington DC, was at the time based at the University of Reading in the UK. In his letter, Kanyama described Kenneth Mwenda's unparalleled academic record as "a rare phenomenon".

Prof Kenneth Mwenda is a leading intellec-tual luminary who, without doubt, ranks amongst the top ten (10) best legal minds that Africa has produced in the twenty-first century. He has taught at some of the best universities in the world, including the University of Warwick in the United Kingdom. He holds a PhD in Law from the said University of Warwick. And who would have imagined that the rare phenomenon referred to by Kanyama in his published letter of 2001 would become rarer with the conferring of a rare Higher Doctorate degree in law (LLD) on Kenneth Mwenda by Rhodes University of South Africa in 2008! Rhodes University, one of the leading universities in Africa, had never in its entire rich history awarded such a distinguished academic award until Kenneth Mwenda received the same. All in all, there are not more than eight (8) to ten (10) eminent African legal scholars with an earned Higher Doctorate degree in Law.

A Rhodes Scholar, Mwenda graduated from, among other institutions, the prestigious Oxford University. In 1998, he turned down a fully funded fellowship to join Yale University Law School, the best law school in the USA, for another competitive offer from the World Bank. It should be noted that the Higher Doctorate degree conferred on Mwenda by Rhodes University in 2008 is a distinguished and rarely awarded senior doctorate. It was awarded after a thorough examination and in recognition of Mwenda's prodigious output of high quality scholarly publications. The story gets even better. Mwenda achieved the rarest academic status in 2014 when he was conferred upon the second Higher Doctorate degree of Doctor of Science in Economics (DSc(Econ)) by a leading British university, the University of Hull. This honour was in recognition of his continued output of highest quality scholarly works, covering both books and peer reviewed articles in leading journals. Hitherto, Mwenda has

- Kenneth K. Mwenda

produced about twenty-five (25) leading books and about ninety (90) journal articles on various subjects, including financial institutions, financial regulation, banking, corruption, corporate governance, diplomatic immunities, public and private international law, money laundering, economic development and related and varied other fields.

Prof. Mwenda's rather as yet not known unique quality and a class by himself is that of public intellectualism whereby he observes everyday life which he then distils into pithy and poignant published metaphors and musings. It is dizzyingly pleasing to read a collection of these metaphors in his latest book which you are holding in your hands. When these self-created "thoughts" were initially sent to me, I thought Mwenda was collecting and circulating other people's sayings until I noted that he had actually thought them and collected them himself. In all cultures, similar sayings are a collection of numerous people's thoughts and ideas and they would have been accumulating over very long periods of time. They are a common heritage of humankind. But in this rare case, Mwenda has sculptured them in his mind all by himself. When you start reading Public Intellectualism and Socio-Political Inquiry through Metaphor and Musing, you will be convinced that Mwenda is one of the greatest public intellectuals of our era, in the company of

Henry Louis Gates Jr.; Cornel West; Ali Mazrui; Wole Soyinka and all those studied in Justice Richard Posner's book entitled, Public Intellectuals. Mwenda's unique intellectualism is also evident in his other publication entitled, Anthology in Law and the Social Sciences in which his commentaries on all conceivable subjects is in full display and a marvel to read. Welcome to a most pleasing roller-coaster ride I have the pleasure of recommending.

Munyonzwe Hamalengwa, PhD
Attorney at Law,

Toronto, Ontario, Canada.
Thursday, April 2, 2015.

PREFACE

While this book does not purport or pretend to have all the answers to the many socio-political challenges that we face in life, it certainly does raise some thought-provoking questions for us to think through. I hasten to add, however, that the book is not a work of fiction. Rather, it is an example of public intellectualism in the Social Sciences. The book distills complex ideas into easily discernible ideas. Such is a cardinal objective of the book – to provoke some critical thinking on topical themes pertaining to socio-political inquiry. This objective is pursued through the use of metaphors and musings. In many cultures, especially those that place much emphasis on oral tradition, knowledge is often handed down to the younger generation through various adages, sayings, metaphors, musings and stories told by the elders to the younger folks around the fire-place. This book attempts to draw from such a tradition, lighting the fire-place and then distilling some untapped wisdom for posterity and the readership.

The writing of the book was prompted by the increasing and growing demand from friends and colleagues for a book that would bring together a collection of some of my notable sayings that I had shared with them over the years on social media or via electronic mail. So, all the sayings contained in this book are not borrowed material, but originally my own. For the reader who is interested in non-original material lifted from other people, you are reading a wrong book. This book is not meant for you. However, for the reader who is interested in reading novel and refreshingly original ideas, this book is meant for you. And you will find a companion in the book. As noted above, the ideas presented in this book are my own.

As a scholar, I have been influenced at various levels of consciousness by the works of many writers and philosophers as well as by many traditions and cultures. And the ideas presented in this book come from a broad spectrum of meta-paradigmatic thoughts that cut across various disciplines in the social sciences. That said, the sound and heartbeat of my work remains my own. Indeed, creative problem-solving requires us to think outside the box. We cannot succeed by using the same models and approaches that led to the very problems that we are trying to solve. We must evolve and adapt. Every system must adapt. It should not be static because change is, ultimately, inevitable. What matters is how we manage that change.

While the book presents an eclectic taste of musings and metaphors, such that many a reader might find it hard to put the book down once they start reading, a deliberate effort is made to set the discussion in its proper socio-political and socio-economic contexts. Much of the analyses are made through the prism of the social sciences. In this book, I endeavor to stand back from my notable scholarly work of authoring for an academic and intellectual audience. What I propose to do instead is to seek dialogue with a broader section of society, ranging from the most intellectually sophisticated to the least enlightened person. Very often, as scholars, our ideas tend to be detached from the real world, particularly when we use technical language and jargon or other forms of communication that only our fellow intellectuals can understand or decipher. Take, for example, the case of a PhD economist who is in the habit of using complex mathematical formula to write or report on contemporary economic issues in the media. How useful is such writing and information to the common man on the ground that has little interest in learning about complex mathematical equations?

A notable role of public intellectualism is to stand back from the intimidating language of a technocrat so as to avoid some kind of tunnel-vision where only you, the author, and your fel-low technocrats are the ones who can understand what you are talking about. And this is exactly what this book endeavors to do. People from different walks of life will find this book an easy read, whether they are travelling on a train or a long flight. The book will give them a valuable companion. And even though some of the readers may not be in full agreement with some of the ideas that the author advances, many a readers' thoughts are likely to be provoked to some greater degree. That, really, is what matters most. Indeed, it is that stimulation of debate that lies at the centre of this book.

A public intellectual often transcends the boundaries of academic pedagogy, while avoiding the chasm that divides scientific inquiry and intellectualism from the typical practitioner role of unscientific advocacy. A public intellectual often remains focused on translating complex theoretical and conceptual ideas into easily discernible scientific and objective analyses that even wananchi (i.e. the public citizens) can understand. In doing so, the public intellectual should try to communicate and speak the language of the common man, without stifling debate or intimidating the audience with all manner of intellectual sophistry. To that end, the use of metaphors, adages, and illustrations becomes handy in breaking down certain ideas that would ordinarily be seen as too complex for the common man to understand. This book takes such an approach, breaking down complex ideas into easily discernible ideas.

This is not a book simply about Africa. Neither is it simply about America or Europe. Rather, the book is about the human condition everywhere in the world.

- *Kenneth K. Mwenda*

We live in a global vil-lage. And the author has lived, studied and worked on three different continents, namely, North America, Europe and Africa. So, every reader will be able to relate to one or more of the sayings, metaphors and musings presented in this book.

Special thanks go to all friends and col-leagues (as well as my family members, including my wife and son) who provided comments on the various sayings, musings and metaphors. Their tireless contributions helped to sharpen my views on a number of issues. Also, my thanks go out to Africa in Canada Press for the timely and efficient publication of the book. And I would be failing in my duties as the author if I did not record my indebtedness to my good brother, Dr. Munyonzwe Hamalengwa, a leading human rights advocate and an outstanding barrister in Canada, for his inspiring Foreword for the book.

The analyses, arguments, interpretations and conclusions expressed in this book are entirely those of the author. They do not represent the views of any institution, person or body to which the author is affiliated.

Kenneth K. Mwenda
PhD, LLD, DSc(Econ).

Washington DC, USA.
Thursday, April 2, 2015.

1

METAPHORS AND MUSINGS

"When all is said and done, and the eu-logies have been offered, the world will begin to move on quickly, with fading memories of yesterday. But the indelible footprints of a man or woman are in his or her ideas. That is the greatest asset that posterity can inherit from us. And so, we must not deny the world of great ideas and thoughts. Great men and women are remembered mostly for their thoughts and ideas."

"The problem with respect is that it will not stay if you keep demanding it with-out earning it."

- Kenneth K. Mwenda

"When we begin to lose sense of who we truly are the only thing that matters is what we want, and not what we de-serve."

"It's a race you must run with courage, fortitude and honor. You cannot afford to be distracted by any naysayers or haters. Let them talk while you forge ahead. If you were not making an impact, they would not be talking. They only talk because you get them worried with your thunder."

"Sometimes, it is not just the number of goals that one has scored that makes him a great soccer player, but also the number of opportunities that he has created for others to score. And that is what true leadership is all about: to make a difference in people's lives."
"If I were to take off my clothes, I doubt that you would see my face. It is not that I will be invisible. Rather, you will be busy looking in the wrong place. People often choose to see in us what they want to see, and not who we are. They are constantly looking for wrong things!"

"People are generally curious. If a pic-ture of your naked self were to come up on social media, it would get the largest number of site visits than one where you are smartly dressed or reading a book in the library. The only issue for the nude picture is that very few people will click the 'like' button for fear of being associated with a dirty mind."

"Sometimes, it is wise just to smile when someone thinks he or she is very clever and has outsmarted you. There are some things that are not worth fighting over. You just have to smile and pretend to be a fool, although you may have seen through the person's wickedness or crookedness. Dishonesty and opportunism, no matter how veiled, only serve to shut the door on those who think they are playing clever when they are not."

"You can admire a culture, attach your-self to the edges of it, and even marry from there, but you are most unlikely to become a part of that culture. It is one thing to acquire a British passport, and another thing to be considered English. Being English, like being French, Amer-ican, African or Asian, is a way of life. It is much more than just holding a foreign passport or marrying into a foreign culture."

"There is nowhere in the world where the Black man has not had to explain himself. Even to his own people, he is often called upon to explain himself."

"They say nothing good can come out of Africa. Many believe it. Don't ask me why. But at every step of the way, they will question you, as an African, to see if you are like the other Africans or are different."

"Some people who come to Africa holding out and pretending to be experts are not really experts. Rather, they are simply charlatans. You must question them, and scrutinize their credentials, in the same manner that they question you or your people in their own countries. Do not be afraid to demand from them evidence of their educational background and work experience."

"Sometimes, we treat people differently, depending on how we have been socialized. I have come to understand that being a foreigner in different parts of the world means different things. In some parts of the world, especially in the Western world, a foreigner, say, from Africa, has to work twice or four times as hard as his or her white European or American counterpart in order to make a mark, if ever he or she will be given a chance. In other parts of the world, especially in many parts of sub-Sahara Africa, a foreigner, say, from Europe or North America, just by virtue of being white, often enjoys preferential treatment by some native and indigenous African people not because he or she is any better than them but because of their own inferiority complex, thinking too highly of him or her."

- Kenneth K. Mwenda

"There are just certain things that we sometimes take for granted only to real-ize that in other societies those same things are either frowned upon or seen as not morally acceptable. In America, you can have a reality show on television showing how well you are living as a celebrity or the mansion you live in as well as the expensive cars you drive. And that's fine. But you cannot do that in some parts of the developing world. It's not alright. Some folks or haters will be up in arms!

In America, you can have a car sticker anywhere on your car that says you went to Harvard. Nobody cares. You can even have a car sticker that says your son is an 'honors student' or the best student at his school. Nobody gives a damn. People simply carry on with their lives, and will not start gossiping about you being arrogant or too full of yourself. It will not bother them one bit. If anything, that might inspire them to do better as well. But just try that on African soil! You know the answer..."

"A notable difference between the life of a musician and that of a scholar is that a musician's life is about breaking the charts whereas a scholar's life is about charting the path."

"There are more gains to be gotten out of giving your precious time to those who, in return, give you their time than wasting your time on those who have no time for you. You cannot win by forcing yourself on people. You are better off with those who appreciate you than those who try to ignore or disrespect you. Once you muster the courage to walk away from the disrespectful lot, they will sober up with the reality that you can do without them."

"When a small child intercepts an elder by helping himself quickly to the biggest portion of meat at the dinner table, you know for sure that the night has been spoiled for the elder. And so it is with life. When someone you thought would never make it far in life rises to the helm of society, it becomes a spoiled night for you."

- Kenneth K. Mwenda

"The wife of a man who, when chewing food, produces disturbing sounds like a locomotive steam engine, with his mouth open and teeth moving like a grinding mortar, or one who, when sip-ping a hot cup of tea, hisses like a spitting cobra, is often at pains to cover up for her husband's embarrassing mu-sical enchantments."

"A gentleman knows fully well that his conversation at the dinner table must not depart from his station in life. He cannot afford to crack crude jokes or laugh out the loudest while clapping his hands from laughter or throwing his legs in the air. He must smile warmly, with a fine demeanor and a measured sense of finesse, etiquette and decorum."

"If I invite you to dinner and begin to talk about political and economic developments internationally, or global warming, it is not that I am boring or trying to show off. Rather, it's simply that I do not intend to talk about peo-ple. At least, you can tell me about the different places where you have been or the different wines that you like if poli-tics and economics is not your cup of tea."

"Do not tell a man who is serious about things that are not serious until you see him relax. Even so, you must be sure not to depart too far from seriousness."

"A gentleman knows fully well that when coming from a dinner date with a fine lady on a cold chilly night, he must surrender his jacket to her so that she stays warm even though he may be gnashing his teeth from the cold. It is still alright, until she tells him that she has to head home to her place, and not to his place. Only a prayer can save his anger and anguish. In life, we should not always expect to get paid for every sacrifice we make."

"If you must invite me to lunch or din-ner, please be considerate enough to turn off your phone and put it away somewhere in your handbag or pocket. I also have a phone."

"It would be unwise to brandish or place conspicuously on the table in front of me your expensive and latest smartphone. I am less impressed by how latest your smartphone is than by how intelligent and honest your conversations are on that phone."

"It is bad manners to shout on top of your voice while on the phone so that everyone around you hears that you are speaking with someone in Paris, France, or London, England, pontificating ma-jestically to everyone nearby to keep quiet since you are busy on an interna-tional call, and chiming in on the phone for all and sundry to hear, 'Hello, how's England? What time is it there? And how's the weather? How I miss Eng-land... Is it snowing already?'"

"If you are not prepared to lose or con-cede any ground, and it's all about you winning everything, you may just end up with nothing. In life, we sometimes must take one step backwards to jump three steps forward."

"I tell you most solemnly that if you must cross the river without a canoe, boat or bridge, then you must be kind and nice to the crocodile to the extent of even allowing that crocodile to tell you about things that you already know, without interrupting it, until you are safely out of the water."

"I ask nothing from you, my friends, but prayers. I only ask for prayers that you may pray for me, and that I too can pray for you. That is all I ask. I know that I am not perfect. So, keep me in your prayers. I shall do the same. Only God knows and sees our hearts. When I am weary and weak because of my love for those close to me, I can only ask God to give me the courage and strength to help them right the wrongs. Because I no longer live for myself alone, but for others as well."

- Kenneth K. Mwenda

"You begin by learning that to be edu-cated entails, among other things, rejecting God because you cannot prove empirically that God exists. Then, you are told that many intellectuals don't believe in God. But life teaches you that there's gotta be something out there that is greater than books and intellect. You begin to understand why money cannot buy you all the happiness or find you all the solutions. You begin to understand why not even political power can save you when your time is up. You sit back in introspection to look at some moments in your life when you knew for sure that the odds were against you, but somehow you miraculously excelled and succeeded. Even those that doubted you could not believe it. And you ask yourself: was that just a coincidence, or was it me just being good at what I do? Then, you know that there's gotta be something out there that science cannot explain. Science has its limits. It cannot explain everything."

"'Oh ye men of little faith, why are you so restless,' says the Lord? 'And why do your hearts get troubled whenever you see a good looking lady? Pray so that you may not be tempted. And fast so that you may be strong in the flesh.'"

"If you pray just to be forgiven for your sins, but not to abate and cease your sinful ways, you are most likely just wasting God's time. There is nothing you have repented, especially if you intend not to cease and abate your sinful ways."

"Do not be obsessed with ranking ahead of others. That is not success. Be obsessed with making a difference. That is the true hallmark of success."

"It worries me that many religious peo-ple choose to pray with one eye open, not wanting to miss out on certain op-portunities in the world. You must choose to have both your eyes closed or open. You can't live a life half in the world and half in the church. Where do you belong? You have to make up your mind."

- Kenneth K. Mwenda

"To pray only when we are in a tight situation or in need of something is not Christianity. We must pray even when not trapped in a tunnel full of smoke. And we must continue to pray whether or not there are rising levels of water threatening to drown us. We ought to pray because of gratitude, and not be-cause of desperation or destitution."

"We are all not perfect. Some people believe in shouting in tongues all day without much being done to uplift the needy. For them, it is all about shouting in tongues inspired by the Holy Spirit. Others believe in a quiet religion while busy with God's work of uplifting the needy through the provision of educa-tional, health and other social services. We can all choose simply to shout alleluia and end there. But our Lord Jesus Christ healed the sick, cast out demons, and did many works in accordance with His faith. Faith and prayer can never be divorced from the realities of life. We do not live or pray in the abstract. There has to be some logical connection between our faith and our deeds. Perhaps, my humble and modest understanding of theology is misplaced and misguided. I don't know."

"From us, the Heavens will demand ev-idence of our good deeds and the acts of love, not just our faith or moving testimonies. It is by our deeds and acts that salvation shall come, and not by our faith alone or the many scriptures that we memorize or quote every day."

"To reduce your age so that you do not retire early from your job, or to claim to have certain qualifications and creden-tials that you do not have in order to get a particular job, is often seen as distasteful and morally wrong. In some jurisdictions, you can be arrested for en-gaging in such practices. However, the more often overlooked case is where someone hides some of his or her quali-fications so that some employer out there does not say he or she is overqualified for the job. Indeed, it is doubtful that such a graceful act of modesty and humility can be described as distasteful and morally wrong. By under-declaring or hiding some of his or her 'big'

quali-fications, the person is simply trying to avoid intimidating some insecure boss and being labeled consequently as over-qualified."

"You should never panic whenever you see a man or woman exuding the smoke of confidence to make you believe that he or she is one of the people that really matter. Some people have now graduat-ed from having airs to causing smoke. You should always look through their smoke. Many insignificant small fires often cause so much smoke, intimidating those without the good training of the eye. here is a difference between real fire and burnt out ashes."

"If you do not know, at least have the humility and appetite to learn instead of masquerading as one who is in the know. A charlatan, no matter how elo-quent, can never be an expert."

"If you don't read widely, you will be-lieve anything that you hear at the hair saloon or the golf club. There is no snow in Zambia, not even malaria in England."

"What matters is what you know, and not what they are telling you. You have eyes to see for yourself."

"The one who comes to tell you that someone was busy saying bad things about you should also tell you what he himself was saying when those bad things were being said. Surely, he did not keep quiet or stay silent throughout the conversation. It is doubtful that he tried to stop the other person from say-ing the bad things. Neither can it be expected that he tried to correct the sit-uation."

"It is folly to expect everyone to like you. There are just too many losers out there who for one reason or another will not like you. It doesn't matter what you do or how much you try to please them. So, just stay the course."

- Kenneth K. Mwenda

"I have come to a realization that one of the most troubling sins that mankind continues to struggle with is jealousy and envy. Most other sins stem from there. Hatred, lies, immorality, theft, murder, and everything else often result from nothing else other than jealousy and envy. You want to have what your friend has even though you have not earned it, or you are not happy that your friend has what you would like to have. It becomes a problem. You begin to plot against him or her. And the first sin committed in the Garden of Eden by Adam and Eve stemmed from the evil one's jealousy and envy of God and His creation. Even our Lord Jesus Christ was both betrayed and crucified because of jealousy and envy. Once you rid yourself of jealousy and envy, you are almost close to a state of purity in Godliness."

"You will know the true worth of a man by how far he can go to make good his promise. Some people have a tendency to throw around cajolery by promising things that they have no capacity or good intent to deliver on. If a man tells you today that he wishes you had sought his help when he was in office, you are surely bound to think that he means well. But should he get a second chance at power, and should you again reach out to him but only to see the man grow cold feet and avoid replying, then you know for sure that he is not a sincere man. Such a man is often not a genuine ally. Life has a way of exposing who your true friends are."

"If I look good, tell me that I look good. Otherwise, I might just have to remind you that I look good. And you won't like me for that. So, it's best you tell me before I say it."

"Jealousy and hatred are like constipa-tion. Once you let go, you feel so relieved. But if you can't let go, you are assured of wild tempers and a debilitat-ing restlessness."

"At common law, a right is an entitle-ment that is often deemed inalienable, requiring no consent or permission from anyone for it to take effect. But the problem with conjugal rights is that they are not enshrined in the Bill of Rights, and remain somewhat in remission at common law, thus raising doubts as to their validity generally, especially in regard to whether or not consent or permission of the other spouse is required before they can be asserted. Western jurisprudence and legal thought seem to require renewed consent every time consummation is about to take effect whereas African customary law seems to proceed on the basis of implied consent throughout the lifespan of the marriage. But those who marry under statutory law cannot claim the benefits of African customary law, especially if their lifestyle has not been governed by some corresponding African custom. Such couples must continually renew their consent and permission when approaching consummation."

"African marriages, or rather marriages contracted under African customary law, are potentially polygamous. But need a man under such a marriage inform his wife or seek her consent to take an additional wife? Probably not, unless an established custom or a piece of legislation so requires."

"Life is sometimes an enigma. A lady with a good heart sometimes ends up with an uncaring, dishonest or unkind man. And a man with a good heart sometimes ends up with a stubborn, ar-gumentative, loud or deeply opinionated lady. Life is never a perfect match, although it can sometimes meet you half way or three-quarters of the way."

"The only problem that I have with the Western concept of human rights is that it jettisons mainly a sense of entitlement, with little regard, if any, to responsibilities and obligations. We cannot just be asking for things that we think we are entitled to without stating or maintaining any corresponding responsibilities or bligations."

"To stand up, without invitation, and say that, 'I agree,' at a meeting that has been called for the nomination of the board chair of a prestigious organization when nobody has nominated you or ex-pressed an intent to nominate you is nothing but utter dishonesty. What are you agreeing to?"

- *Kenneth K. Mwenda*

"It would be unwise to disclose to a man's children that although their father keeps telling them that he was the best student in school, you were actually a better student. If you were to make such a disclosure, it would break their innocent hearts. It is best to let the children believe the pitiful lies told by their father. For, a lie is sometimes kinder than the truth."

"You can have all the money in this world, but if, at midnight, you should need to use the toilet and then discover that there is no toilet paper, not even your money can save you. If you were to force matters using some of your cash money, you may end up injuring yourself. In life, everyone we meet is important. We should not just focus on those with money, fame and power. We might need some of that toilet paper one day."

"I have seen so many wealthy but ugly looking men date some of the prettiest ladies in town. But I have not seen many highly intelligent and not that bad looking men succeed at dating such pretty ladies. I don't know why."

"If your neighbor's dog eats the chicken that you have been raising for your much awaited Christmas meal it does mean that you should now beat the dog mercilessly or force a boiling egg into its mouth. You must talk to your neighbor to ensure that he feeds his dog, especially that he is in no position to lend you another chicken. Something that will be eaten cannot be borrowed."

"Women must understand that a man cannot keep putting fuel in a car that he does not drive. The man that drives the car must put fuel in it. Men, too, must understand that they cannot expect to drive a car that they have not put fuel in. The man that has put fuel in it must drive the car."

"If I meet you for the first time, and you introduce yourself to me as Ms. XYZ, that is, the surname of your former husband who you have now divorced, do not get upset when I begin to ask you innocently about how he is doing. You had better drop that name before I ask too many questions that might end up upsetting you."

"From a Christian point of view, dating a divorced man is just as adulterous as dating a married man. There is absolutely no difference. Under Christianity, there is generally no such thing as divorce when you are married. The only exception under which divorce is permitted is where a female spouse is guilty of adultery. Otherwise, any sexual encounter outside the original marriage by a purportedly divorced person is simply adultery no matter how much he or she may try to justify the act by making it seem alright."

"The unpleasant part about dating a married man is that he may not leave his wife any time soon, although you may have a good time with him. But, at least, you both know where you stand. Contrastingly, that does not make a single guy any better an option. The unpleasant part about dating a bachelor is that you just don't know how many other women he has told those same lies to that he wants to mar-ry them. For him, he has an endless bait to throw at so many women. It is hard to even know his whereabouts at times because he can be anywhere at any time. And you may not know where you stand with him until he decides to marry; that is, if you are the lucky one."

"There is something 'prostitutional,' if I may say, about people who change too often their choice of churches, political parties, jobs, careers, professions, and other relationships, including their choice of women, men, wives, hus-bands, and friends. It is hard to trust such people for they smack of instabil-ity, disloyalty, dishonor and unpredictability. Loyalty is often wanting as an attribute in their character. For them, expediency is the mantra, often predicated on self-serving interest."

"If a man does not marry 'well', mean-ing if he knows that his choice of a wife is not very satisfactory, he will often not talk about his wife. You should understand his silence."

"A woman will often not admit that she left her man because he no longer has money. Rather, she will say that he lacks initiative, is not resourceful, hardly provides for the family and is very irresponsible. You must figure out the euphemisms."

"There is a marked difference between trusting and understanding. To trust, you must believe whereas to understand you don't necessarily have to believe. The reason why so many people get heartbroken at times is because they trust a fellow human being too much. It is best simply to understand a fellow human being, and to reserve all our trust for the God we believe in."

"Mistaking sex for love is one of the biggest challenges facing much of to-day's young generation. You cannot decide to marry or get married just be-cause of sex or lust. You will be bored very quickly. After all, an orgasm doesn't last long. Marriage is far much more than that. It requires character. Those without character often fall on the side easily."

"You must not get upset when your friend is in love with your aunt or your sister. After all, you will not marry either of them. Simply advise them to stay out of harms-way to avoid becoming regrettable and pitiful victims."

"If, as a father or mother, one of your friends were to end up dating your beautiful adult daughter, it is best to check with the police first whether or not he has committed any wrong or broken any law before you do anything seriously wrong that could land you in prison."

"If your wife or girlfriend is very attrac-tive and good looking, be assured that you are not the first and only man to have noticed that.

- Kenneth K. Mwenda

But it should not cause you to panic when other men look at her. Simply focus on your agenda."

"A wise man does not go about issuing threats to a fellow man, warning him to stay away from his wife or girlfriend. Rather, he knows full well that it is best just to deal with the said wife or girl-friend so that she stops entertaining the other man."

"A man that often snoops into his wife's or girlfriend's emails, or social media chats and postings, taking stock of the men communicating with her or liking her postings, is often an insecure man and may eventually start to lose weight from unnecessary worry. A lot of men on social media will continue to like her lovely and sexy-looking pictures, and the sooner he comes to term with this the better."

"Cultures differ globally. In some cul-tures, young people inherit serious wealth from their parents. In our case, we often inherit only blessings, and sometimes wisdom too. And that is why we often don't believe in writing wills. Blessings don't have to be in a will."

"The advantage of age in the developing world, including Africa, Asia, and Latin America, is that anyone younger than you is not expected to ask you tough questions."

"Many an African parents, including those that can barely afford to send their children abroad for undergraduate university education, shun local universities in Africa as not good enough for their children. I, like many other African scholars in the diaspora, have at times found myself teaching African students at a Western university, although I actually took my undergraduate studies in one of the very African universities that some African parents and children shun. Isn't it ironic that some people can travel so many miles to go and study abroad, and only to be taught by a fellow African who graduated from that same local African university that they are trying to shun, notwithstanding his or her postgraduate education from abroad.

Even when our politicians are some-times rushed to South Africa for specialist medical treatment, some of the so-called specialist medical doctors there are from the same African politicians' native countries, having qualified first as medical doctors at their home university medical school(s) before pursuing foreign-based postgraduate training.

Why do we often want to rush to some foreign country, especially a seemingly more developed one, or overseas, before we try our own expertise locally?"

"A person that has grown up with the luxury and affluence of an expensive whiskey at his disposal does not go around repeating to people that he had just taken two shots of whiskey early in the day, unless he has only graduated recently from some habitual indulgence in less finer drinks."

"If I were to compliment you for your lovely dress, handbag or shoes, it does not mean that you should now start singing me a medley of where you bought it from, the brand name, or how much it cost you. All that is expected from you is a simple 'Thank you'."

"For many parents, what is deemed a good school to take their children to is simply where the rich and the affluent take their kids. Even when people talk of a good hospital or clinic, it is simply where the rich and the affluent get admitted to or seek treatment from. Our standards are often skewed and influenced mainly by the bizarre tastes of the supposedly wealthy."

"To tell friends and colleagues confidently that you will be traveling abroad for Christmas holidays when you will be going to the village to visit your grandma is not the safest thing to do. You might be on the same early morning intercity bus with your neighbor, as she travels to attend a family wedding. Neither can you lock yourself indoors at home and avoid answering any phone calls at Christmas time. Your creditors might just be at your doorpost to grab some properties for the unsettled debts. You must answer their call or else..."

"One who says she just attended a lousy wedding ought to tell us if at all she ever had a wedding herself as well as how great or good it was. And one who says the marrying groom is just a jerk ought to tell us if at all her man is any better, that is, if at all she has a man. By parity of reasoning, one who says that the bride is not all that ought to tell us if at all his own bride was any better."

"When your neighbor puts up a Christ-mas tree with all the fancy lights and hang-ons that come with it, and the neighbor's children are busy bragging to your children about their lovely Christ-mas tree, getting your children unnecessarily and visibly worried or dis-turbed, you know that it's time for you to up the game.

It won't help to try to explain to your children to let it go."

"You cannot live your life constantly trying to compare what you have with what others have. Life is not, and should not be, like that. Otherwise, if we all started comparing, some of us would end up as the Secretary-General of the United Nations, based on our superior academic qualifications. But life is not like that. Once you begin to appreciate, value and use the talents that God has given you, then you are on the path to a greater fulfillment and satisfaction. It's all about knowing your strengths and talents, and not worrying about your neighbor's strengths or talents. And if you insist on comparing, then take a look at your neighbor's weaknesses so as to appreciate your strengths."

"I miss the olden days of the famous hun-ger strikers in the 1980s, and not this human violence and terrorism that the world is witnessing nowadays. Back then, courageous and determined individuals would go on peaceful hunger strike predi-cated on their moral conviction to express dissent or force a government to make a policy shift. Some hunger strikers would even die from the hunger eventually. These were principled people who would not relent or trade their convictions for anything else. But today, everyone everywhere is scared and worried about human violence and suicide bombers. Why have we become so violent as a people? What do we gain out of violence?"

"To be excited because you got ninety-eight percent (98%) in an exam is miss-ing the point. Where is the other two percent (2%)?" "We must understand that in every country there is at least five to ten minutes or more when there is, techni-cally speaking, no head of state because he or she is not capable at that moment to make any well-reasoned decisions until his or her faculties are back to normalcy."

"The journey of a good man is a journey of genuine sacrifice. He will make sacri-fices even for those who, if they were in his shoes, would not make those same sacrifices for him. Do not expect every-one you help to say 'thank you' or to be there for you when you need their help."

"A local superstar or local champion must understand that splashing water in his or her local bathtub is not the same thing as swimming across the shark and crocodile infested international waters of this world. You must have character to last against the high tides of the oceans and the seas. By contrast, there are hardly any sharks, crocs or tides in the local bathtub. All you have is bathing soap."

"Very often, those who are quick at advising their friends to leave their marriage and walk away from their man have themselves not demonstrated such courage or bravery de-spite having lived through similar challenges. The only difference here is that they never say the type of hell that they have been through, making you think or believe that their marriages are perfect. Not even the guy who advises you to quit your job when things are not looking good at work has ever quit his job. He is busy toiling in that same old job, yet trying to tell you lies about better prospects out there!"

"I cannot pick up the phone just to tell you that XYZ has been fired from his or her post. Neither can I pick up the phone to tell you that ABC's marriage is on the rocks. I will not pick up the phone to ask you if you have passed the exams when I know already that you did not do well. Yet, day in and day out, we have many people, including some seemingly holier than thou Christians, who thrive on such negativity. By contrast, I will share with you the good news that XYZ has just been appointed to an esteemed position or has just passed his or her exams with flying colors so that we can all celebrate and be inspired. And I will share the good news that ABC has just gotten married so that we can all be delighted for the couple and give them our blessings. That, to me, is what makes a difference, and it tells you who I am."

"The one who is often saying bad things about you surely loves you but in a wrong way. It is a wrong kind of love in the sense that he or she cannot have you or have the things that you have. Or, it could be that he or she cannot do the things that you have done or continue to do, or cannot reach the heights that you have reached. The only thing left is to vent anger. And anger, fueled by jealousy or possessiveness, is a form of negative love."

"As Christmas approaches, I pray that you, my friends, may walk not into the snares and traps of that King Herod who has been smiling at you while wait-ing eagerly to do you in. For there are too many King Herods in our lives and amongst those we consider our friends and allies, with some showing false allegiance yet full of hearts of treachery. I pray that God protects you from your King Herod as He, God, protected the Baby, our Lord Jesus Christ, from King Herod of the time when Herod told lies to the wisemen that he too wanted to go and pay homage and worship the messiah. Yet Herod's heart was overflowing with envy, jealousy, insecurity and hatred that a newly born child would ultimately steal his thunder. May God send the three wisemen through the guardian angels to protect you all from the insecurities and hatred of your King Herods while you are at work, home, traveling or wherever else you could be. May the wise men lead you safely through an unexpected route that is unknown to King Herod. There are just too many King Herods out there, waiting to do you in or to see you fall. But God is great, and He shall not let you down."

"When a people are poor, anyone can sell them anything, including what is believed to be the Holy Spirit. Many poor people have been sold various religious dogma and foreign languages, without ever questioning the value of such ideological constructs. Some poor people are even made to fight amongst themselves and to discriminate against one another based on those inherited colonial languages and foreign religions. Should it really matter which African speaks French or English? And does it matter which church you go to, or which religion you belong to, when you all just inherited those religions? Others have been sold names, making them believe that they can only get baptized using a Western name. Being poor is a terrible thing. As Karl Marx once said, matter determines consciousness. Even a magician can delude you into believing in false miracles simply because of your destitution and desperation. But with a bit of intellect or wisdom, God willing, you can come out of it."

"The problem with religion without educa-tion is that it sometimes leads to extremism and dogmatism. Unenlightened forms of reli-gion or religiosity, claiming to rely only on the Holy Spirit, are dangerous. They must be avoided, if at all possible.

And the problem with education without a diverse cultural exposure and with limited travel is that the knowledge acquired does not often sit in the right political, economic and social contexts. Quite often, it ends up just as an academic degree on the wall. Traveling by itself, like cultural exposure, is additional knowledge. It helps to make one appreciate things differently and from differ-ent perspectives. A well-educated European or American, for example, who has never been to Africa is likely to be blinded by the same type of public media prejudices en-countered by a well-educated African who has not been to the other side of the Atlantic Ocean. They both need exposure."

"If you don't clap, a man will not get off the stage. He will keep trying even if you boo him. You must clap hard so that he may think he has done exceedingly well, and that will get him off the stage quickly and amicably."

"Politics is like toilet paper. If you go in there blindly, they will sometimes use you, and then flush you down the sewer. It's hard to recover from such an experience because nobody sensible enough wants to have a go at used and recycled toilet paper."

"As a leader, you ought to know that when people are no longer listening to you, it is time to listen to them."

"When politicians are busy jostling for power, they want to make the world believe that it is the 'people' that are not happy or who are really suffering. Yet, the truth is that it is the politicians themselves, especially those in the opposition, that are most unhappy for not being in power and who are really suffering from the envy they harbor of those in power. Do not let politicians mislead you. The actual 'people' are different from the politicians. And the respective interests of the people and the politicians are different. Let the politicians fight their own battles without dragging you, the people, into the mud with them."

"The problem with being a follower, and not a leader, is that when the leader starts a fight you have to finish off the fight for him. All he has to do is start the fight. How you finish off that fight is your business. Sometimes, even before he starts the fight, you have to confront his adversaries and start the fight on his behalf. It is the same in politics. Those in power must, on behalf of their president, fight off any of his adversaries even where the president is, himself, fast asleep or relaxing and enjoying a cup of coffee. They must fight on his behalf mercilessly even though they may not know the origins of the conflict."

"In the art of persuasion, you win by in-fluencing outcomes rather than by using force. Even where legal authority, or other forms of authority, help to influ-ence a desired outcome, such authority is usually earned rather than imposed on the subjects. As such, persuasion is a natural ally of legitimacy whilst force and ideology are adopted allies. Alt-hough force and ideology may win you legitimacy, the deployment of persua-sion hardly ever demands legitimacy. Rather, legitimacy comes as a natural ally and at a lesser cost."

"Once an intellectual becomes partisan with his ideological views, it is hard to maintain objectivity in the analytical discourse. As thought leaders, we must draw a line between our subjective political preferences and the objective imperative."

"If you do not hear me say much about domestic policies and politics in my na-tive country, it is not because I do not care. And it is not because I am afraid. Neither is it because I want to please anyone or to sit on the fence. Far from it. Rather, it is because I am often pre-occupied with international development issues at the global level that will eventually feed into the domestic policies of the same countries that we all care for."

"That I do not pick up a megaphone spiritedly to air my political grievances to all and sundry does not mean that I have betrayed the cause of the people. We all can't be activists. There are those who know best only how to talk and verbally attack personalities. Then, there are those who work quietly with the people through various services to a country's institutions. We all must build, and not divide, a country or people. That is our civic responsibility. But with insults, we cannot help much in developing a country. It is in working with people that we can make a difference."

- Kenneth K. Mwenda

"I have told my wife that if, or rather when, I become the president of my na-tive country, Zambia, she should not form a charity organization akin to those formed by some First Ladies in Africa which eventually become obsolete and redundant the moment their husbands are no longer in power. We must move away from such mentalities. And for some former First Ladies, it takes a while for them to come to terms that they can no longer call the shots as they did when their spouse was in power."

"Many an African parents, especially the fathers, hardly apologize to their children when they are wrong. If anything, it is considered disrespectful to remind an African father that he is wrong. You must all just keep quiet and suffer in silence at his many mistakes. And that approach is extrapolated by many at the political level, elevating the African presidency into a parental role over the citizenry, thus affirming the African president as the 'wise' father of the nation."

"You must not try so hard to impress or to make an impression. Rather, you must work hard to excel. And when you excel, you won't need extra effort to im-press or to make that impression. It just comes naturally."

"As a fable would show, a dog following a trickster of a hare gets stuck at the neck as it tries desperately to go through a narrow tunnel. The dog was following the hare blindly without realizing the limitations ahead. The hare went through the tunnel safely whilst the dog remained stuck. This fable demonstrates what happens often in real life when some people try to follow others blindly just because they believe, rightly or wrongly, that the other folks are the people that matter. It is always safe and best to be your own man or lady, with your own independent mind and identity."

"If you must shine, it is not good to shine just for one minute. Otherwise, the others might outshine you when it matters most. You must always think long-term, and not just in terms of short-term thunder."

"It is unwise to embark on some agenda just to prove a point to someone. You can't live your life constantly trying to prove a point to someone. And you don't have to be bitter with the world when others seem to be doing better than you, especially those that you may have once looked down upon. You just have to live your life within your means and be happy."

"Back in the day, if one were to be taken seriously as an intellectual or scholar worth listening to, there was no escaping from a good grounding in leftist ideology. And so, many of us read a lot of that in the formative years of our intellectual life. Indeed, Marxist-Leninist ideologies, including the Afrocentric versions of the same, are what defined a scientific argument then. I have no regrets that I spent many years immersing myself intellectually in leftist ideas. It is always best to know about something than not to know. You cannot convince me about the wrongfulness of something when you hardly know a meaningful thing about it. To me, that intellectual grounding helped to shape my thinking and understanding of issues at a whole different philosophical level. Yet, I am neither a Marxist nor a radical. Rather, I am a pragmatist who is sympathetic to the plight of the poor and the under-privileged as well as one whose ideas are shaped by a broad spectrum of different ideological bases and experiences."

"People have a tendency to draw wrong conclusions before you even finish talk-ing. If, for example, you were to be half way in a sentence, and were to say something like, 'One is smaller than the other...' (Bemba translation: 'Limo li nono pali nankwe...'), they will often run quickly to the most perverse and disturbing thoughts. Yet, you could be talking about one tooth (ilino) or eye (ilinso) being smaller than the other. We must be open-minded enough to listen to what others are saying."

"It may sound controversial and unpop-ular, but it is irresponsible for a biological father or mother of a child to show up only later in the child's life when the child is all grown up and doing well. Such a person should not try to take credit for the successes of his or her son or daughter to a point of even wanting to overshadow the step-parent or extended family member(s) that helped in raising the child. If you were not there as a parent, then you were not just there. You are simply not a parent but merely a biological father or mother. God will judge you fairly. You don't father children and walk away like an unschooled and uncultured thief. You must take up responsibility in raising the child and show maturity."

"One who decides to wed must not look to the pockets of his relatives, friends or in-laws. He made the marital choice alone. Therefore, for every benefit that he shall take shall come responsibility, unless he were to allow others to partake in the benefits or fruits of his marriage."

"If I were to ask you innocently, as a friend, who you are dating, engaged to or planning to marry, or even about the identity of the father of your lovely in-nocent child, do not tell me that, 'ulya mwana ba kantwa...ta mwa beshiba?' (Eng-lish translation: 'the son of that famous man or politician...you should know the man'). Rather, tell me about the guy himself, and not his parents or relatives. I want to know or hear about his CV, and not that of his parents or relatives."

"In life, as you grow older and mature, your points of historical reference grad-ually shift away from your primary or elementary school experiences as well as from your middle or high school experiences to much more academically established experiences. For the most part, your college or university experi-ence becomes the more pronounced historical reference, unless you are still stuck in the past. And that is why for many people their CVs do not carry the name of the high school they attended, or the grades or points they obtained at high school. You start with the college or university that you attended, and the rest follows from there."

- *Kenneth K. Mwenda*

"To get ahead, you don't have to throw anyone underneath the bus. The bus driver may just swerve the bus into your path, as he tries desperately not to run over the innocent victim."

"You can't keep telling people that, 'You don't know me? I am former Vice-President' or 'former CEO', when eve-ryone else has moved on, and there are new kids on the bloc. The sooner you realize that the word 'former' is not a job title, the better. Former simply means there is nothing to talk about in the present age."

"Some people's pride, overzealousness and ambition often exceeds their abili-ties and potential, deluding even the well-qualified and competent into be-lieving that such people are the best choice for the job. You have to have a trained eye to spot them. And you will never hear them talk about school, what they studied or where they studied. All they talk about are the big names of prominent people that they know or the things that they own."

"In life, if you are too ambitious and unapologetically overzealous, wanting to get to the top at all costs, with your eyes and mind focused only to the North of life's compass, you will miss the East and the West, and end up in the South."

"Some people are too ambitious to a point that they only talk to individuals that they think will influence their business agenda or career path to greater heights. They will not waste their time talking to, dining with or having a coffee with someone they consider immaterial to the advancement of their career path or business goals. That's a notable difference between a corporate hustler or commercial thug, on the one hand, and a decent person, on the other. Sadly, many decent people with edifying values of integrity don't go too far in the corporate world."

"Some people are just too proud. Even when they would like to talk to you, they will first pretend as if they have not seen or noticed you, waiting and hoping that you will be the one to reach out to them. On social media too, some old friends or acquaintances behave like that, constantly visiting your social media page while waiting to see if you will send them a friend request until they see that none is forthcoming. Life is too short to be playing games. Just be happy and get on with life without unnecessary hang ups."

"A lady that looks away when you catch her stealing a glance at you must just say hello, without pretending not to have noticed you. It is obvious she has been checking you out. How you react when someone catches you looking at them or when your eyes meet with their eyes says a lot about your inner thoughts."

"The problem with dealing with a beau-tiful lady is that she is very likely to know that she is beautiful. To win her over, you do not need to overstate or belabor the point about her beauty. Many people have been telling her the same thing. Rather, it is wise to take her into a different but pleasant zone that she is not familiar with."

"I have met many international and em-inent persons. And I have met several heads of state, and dined with some of them. I even met Dr. Nelson R. Man-dela as well as Col. Muammar Ghadaffi. Sitting with Col Ghadaffi and discussing international issues on a one-on-one, with a man that was most feared internationally even by the West, remains a memorable and indelible experience. I have also shared intellectual platforms with some of the most respected international thought leaders and scholars out there. And I have had the honor to sit and dine with Dr Kenneth Kaunda, one of the pioneering and founding fathers of Africa. In all this, I have learned many things. But I cannot stop without sharing the most humane experience and feeling that I get whenever I work with very poor people and with young people in universities around the world. It's never about money, power or fame, but about the people."

"Depending on your level of profes-sional and intellectual sophistication as well as your international exposure, the names that you think really matter in society may not be the same as the names that impress the other person. Do not get surprised if I tell you that I do not know, and have never heard of, the man that you are busy falling all over for, and one over whom you are panicking excitedly. He may not be a factor to me. If anything, it is better that you ask him about me, and not you asking me about him. The point is that some of the people that you follow as newsmakers are likely to be different from the people that I follow. To understand what moves me, you may have to pay close attention to my ideas and thoughts. Some people get moved easily by names that are not a factor. Others get moved by local names known only locally within the local neighborhood or local tabloids. Some people are simply too basic in their outlook to life. It is best to look at substance and not form."

"If you should decide to date or marry, it is wise to avoid dating or marrying someone who you constantly have to keep explaining to people or making ex-cuses for. Eventually, you might get tired of doing so. If he can't read or write, just say so. If he lacks table man-ners, just leave him at home. If she is a drama queen, keep your distance until nightfall. You can't keep covering up for such people. Sooner or later, the waiter attending to both of you will ask that person to place an order from the menu card, and you may not have the chance to cover for him or her. If he can't read, he just can't read. Neither can he keep saying he will have the same food or drink as you every time you go out. People will eventually notice, especially if he has his newspaper upside down, pretending to be reading."

"Some people's lives are just too full of problems. To fall in love with them is to inherit problems. To marry them is to marry problems. And to walk away from them is to walk away from problems. Be careful with the type of person you fall in love with or choose to marry. You may end up with and in problems."

"The problem with people who like to borrow money or take goods on credit is that they often have too many stories to tell. And their stories often don't make sense."

"To choose willfully to forget, or to shut your eyes recklessly to, those who carried you during your hard times or when you needed help most is a clear reflection of your true character. It does not matter how many Bible verses you quote to others every day. Those who complain that they do not like being held indebted to a person forever just because he or she helped them are often simply ungrateful people. If you can show gratitude, the person is less likely to remind you of how he or she helped and carried you. Only when you try to pretend not to have been helped will you be reminded. So, it is easier to show gratitude than not to."

"I often wait until someone finishes saying bad things about another person before I ask him or her how that will benefit or help me. Almost always, it throws them off-balance."

"If you tell off someone, and they go to tell other people that you are a bad per-son, they are being insincere and dishonest. They have not said why you told them off, but simply want to paint you as a bad or crazy person. People must learn to tell the whole truth, and not reciting mere conjectures or anec-dotes of fiction and facts."

"Every time they tell you that someone is a difficult person and not easy to work with, ask them if they themselves are that easy to work with and are not in any way difficult, especially that by bringing up such gossip they are confirming that they are actually difficult people. Until you see for yourself, it would be naive to believe what they are saying. You might end up hating on a good person just because of the sour grapes that they are feeding you with."

"Some people never see any good in others. If honor is bestowed on some-one else, and not them, such people will complain and criticize those that are honored. For them, it is only they who deserve the honor, and not others. Life teaches us that those who are so egocentric and self-centered in their approach to life often end up isolated, lonely and bitter, no matter how much they may try to congratulate themselves. To rise up every morning with destructive selfishness only leaves you exhausted at night as you go to sleep. And the next morning, you wake up lonely, isolated and bitter to start hating all over again. Life should not be like that. We can all do better if we can move away from the destructive path of selfishness."

"An adult who pretends to be in the know when, in actual fact, he or she does not know is like a child who, at night, refuses to go to sleep, struggling hard to stay awake in front of a televi-sion set while protesting vehemently that he or she is very much awake. Sooner or later, it will show."

"Where I come from, in particular under African customary law, if a man were to die with unkempt and unshaven pubic hair, his wife would be held fully accountable not for his death but for allowing his pubic hair to grow and mushroom uncontrollably. And the concepts of causation or foreseeability in Western jurisprudence do not matter. It is irrelevant that she did not cause his pubic hair to grow or that she did not foresee his untimely death before she could shave his pubic hair. Strict liability applies immediately."

"You can ask an American man or Eu-ropean man about his funeral insurance, but do not ask an African man about the same. The African man will immediately panic, thinking that you want to bewitch him, poison him or do something drastically bad to him."

"Admitting that you do not know, or that you lack the relevant knowledge, on a particular subject or topic is the first step in the process of learning. Making such an admission need not be seen or taken as a weakness or loss of face, but as an act of courage and character. For one who is self-conceited with vanity and the unyielding ego of pride hardly ever learns."

"Time is always never enough. I know that life is a journey, taking us to various places, known and unknown. But there is always a place big enough in our hearts to love even though time may sometimes deny us to meet when I have only a few days to visit my motherland."

"If you must find a role model, do not sit with people who constantly hate on others. If you look at them carefully, such people are nowhere close to the person they are criticizing or hating. And that tells you something about them and why they sound bitter. A pro-gressive person has no time to hate on others. And that explains why he or she is ahead of them."

"Some people have difficulties distinguishing the word 'fixing' from the word 'damaging'. By harboring hatred against someone, or plotting revenge or some vendetta of some kind, and claiming that you are going to fix someone, you are actually doing the exact opposite. You are plotting to damage, and not to fix. Damaging and fixing are two different things. Only medical doctors, and not someone who is upset or angry, can fix people."

"The world is changing. A lot of women are earning more money than men. And several women are getting a much higher education than men. Besides, some women are now the main breadwinners in their homes and relationships. Men can no longer continue to feel entitled to authority, especially where they have not earned the authority. You must earn your authority, whether as a man or a woman. Otherwise, you have no choice but to salute the one in authority."

"Do not assume that the lady you are talking to is the secretary or assistant to the person that you are looking for or should be seeing just because she is a woman. Indeed, she may just turn out to be the person that you need to talk to, or she could be the boss. And do not assume that a lady is a medical nurse, and not a medical doctor, just because she is a woman or is young. You may end up getting a shock of your life. Be open-minded. A woman can do anything that a man can do professionally."

"If you do not see my footprints amongst much social and political con-temporary, it is not that the footprints have faded away. You are simply looking at the wrong trail because God has carried me on a different path. And that path requires no noise, but an edifying sense of quiet."

"I only drop my left hook when I know that my right hand has done its work. You must first create fertile conditions for an enabling environment before you can make a move. Otherwise, you will be laboring in vain."

"In anything you would like to be or pur-sue in life, whether it has to do with education, wealth, fame or faith, you must first believe in yourself. Without that belief, you will forever be speculating."

"If you know that you need someone in your life, you had better have fewer opin-ions or keep them to your own self. Uku sunga imbwa mano, te mu chipyu iyo. Kuti ya butuka po fye (i.e. even a dog may run away if you are constantly mistreating it with opinionated harshness)."

"Every day, we wake up with opinions and go to sleep with opinions. That's why we sometimes can't get along. We each have too many opinions. But our respective opinions are not necessarily factually true."

"Pay attention to those who will admit that they've got it wrong or missed the point, and will get back to the drawing board. Pay attention also to those that admit that they never thought of it in the manner it has been explained until you said it. Pay attention to those who will admit that they do not know and, thus, seek some guidance. And pay at-tention to those that are magnanimous enough to say that they would like to learn how it works or how things are done. Pay attention also to those that admit that they are sinners, and seek God's forgiveness and grace. But when it comes to those that have appointed themselves as self-righteous, standing on a pedestal of an ever-right mer-chant of morals or an unbending debater that always wants to win an argument in a vested or self-interested egoistic manner, you need not worry. They could be going through things of their own or could be embattled with issues. Theirs is not knowledge, but destructive pride."

"You must understand that sometimes the haters will not hesitate to raise alarm in the man or woman that you are growing to like and are just about to start dating, telling him or her that two or three of the men or women that dated you have since died. And when your lover-to-be gets to hear that, it may not make much difference that you only dated one man or woman who died from a car accident."

"It is criminal not to disclose to the one you are about to get closely intimate with the actual cause of death of your former lover or what he or she is suffer-ing from, especially if that illness can affect your new lover. There is a duty of care at common law to disclose all material facts, or simply to stay away from any new relationship to avoid any disclosures. You can't keep hiding the truth. Neither can you tell lies or half-truths that the person just died from a sudden unknown illness. By parity of reasoning, to claim that the deceased was bewitched when you know what he or she died from is simply doing gross injustice to your new partner. It is not helpful also to point only at a secondary illness while knowing full well the nature of the underlying primary illness that could have triggered the secondary illness. You must tell the truth."

"It does not take much to be famous. Just do or say something silly or crazy. Everyone will be talking about you and the stupid things that you did or said. You will be all over the news. But if you want to be a respected or renowned person, the formula is rather slow and hard to come by.

You need a lot of patience and hard work to break the ceiling."

"It is estimated that in one's lifetime, some people will have had sex many more times than they will have picked up a book to read. It's a global tragedy. Others will have drunk more glasses of alcohol than the number of books that they have seen in their lifetime, or smoked more cigarettes than the total number of pages that they have skimmed through in their entire life. What a life!"

"A restless and impatient man often loses his erection quickly."

"People get into marriages or relation-ships for various reasons. Some look for an economic messiah in the marriage or relationship. But since the great times of Abraham and Moses, the world no longer has messiahs. Other people look for prophets of love. Some look for guardian angels. But since the advent of money in this world, we have commer-cialized love. It is hard to find these prophets or guardian angels. Without money, love is threatened even amongst family and friends. Today, there are more divorce cases, concubines, and mistresses in the urban areas than they were, say, in the traditional African vil-lage set-up many years ago when money was not an issue. We must face up to reality. The love of money has corrupted this world badly."

"There is no such thing as an ugly man. The looks of a man are often defined by his wallet. Quite often, you must look inside his wallet to see how handsome he is."

"One thing about money is that it can make you look good even though you may not be that good looking. And it can win you fame and followers. But it can never make you sound knowledgeable, unless you have that knowledge."

"Do not be cheated. We live in a materialistic world. Whether we like it or not, money plays a notable role in the choices we make as well as in the circle of friends or family members that we have. Even the definition of love has a monetary connotation attached to it today. We cannot pretend. And so, those that cannot afford to maintain a lady must not waste her time. Rather, let those with the means step up to the challenge. Even in marriage, you must ensure that your beloved wife is well maintained and loved to reflect your standing and standards as a man of substance. Otherwise, people will question your station in life if you cannot maintain your wife and children to the level of your own standards."

"Because we live in a materialistic world, we often like to cite and recite only names of supposedly well-to-do or affluent family members whenever we are asked about our families. The names of the most seemingly wealthy sibling, cousin, aunt or uncle often sit comfortably on the pecking order of the citations or recitations. Other relatives or siblings, especially the poor ones, are not mentioned at all."

"You will have more 'friends' and 'rela-tives' in spending than in saving. People like to hang out with those that can spend, as opposed to those that are busy saving."

"In some jurisdictions, it is a criminal offense to obtain marriage by false pre-tenses. An individual that commits the offense will have deceived the victim by, say, making false and misleading representations that she is of a naturally light complexion when, in actual fact, she is not but for cosmetic skin-complexion enhancing creams, or that he is of such a high station in life or of high intellect when, in actual fact, he is simply an undischarged bankrupt, a charlatan or some unscrupulous character, with or without, fixed abode."

"Of our ethnic group or race, you can only tell the true and original skin com-plexion of a person by looking at her knuckles, ankles, knees, elbows and butt area. Those areas never lie."

"If, as soon as we step into the night-club, you must pretend that you have forgotten your wallet at home, telling me that you need a short loan to massage the situation, I will call you a cab to take you home to get the wallet."

"A man enjoying a beer in the company of friends who rises up from his seat to head to the toilet, pretending to feel pressed, when he knows that it is now his turn to buy a round of beers for the others is not smart enough. It is wise to wait for him to return from his indulgences before inviting the bartender to take the order from him."

"Those who hardly buy beers when in the company of others, but would rather drink free beers off another person's budget must not think that people have not noticed them. Make no mistake about that. Your friends have already noticed but are just polite enough to let it go so as not to embarrass you. And so it is with all manner of selfishness. That people have not said anything does not mean that they have not noticed your selfish and self-centered behavior. They are just watching you, and you'd better change before you get embarrassed by a tell-off from someone."

"In cultures that are fraught with suspi-cion, whenever you are trying to explain a simple idea or concept, some people begin to suspect that you are up to no good. Others assume wrongly that you could be talking about them. And so, some people will be unusually quiet, held down with discomfort, before in-terjecting spiritedly, 'Ninshi mwalosha mwisa ifyo mwasosa?' (i.e. '...just what ex-actly are you trying to say?'). Very often, lack of trust defeats the whole purpose of a meaningful conversation."

"Everywhere you go, people do not like to be asked historical questions about their troubled past, especially if the past casts them in a negative light. But they will be quick to remind you how great they were in those areas of the past where they thrived."

"The easiest way to lose 'friends' is to be very honest and frank about issues. Many are not ready for that. If anything, they tend to be so sensitive to the truth, worrying unnecessarily that you tend to talk with so much emphasis."

"Those ladies that, for economic rea-sons, are in the habit of eating heavy food at home before going out to the club rarely do that when a man offers to take them out somewhere on a date. Rather, they will show up very hungry, and order the most expensive food or something that they have never eaten before but have just been admiring from afar. It does not take long before a man notices. Remember to be yourself and to be considerate even if you are not the one paying for the food or service. That way, you will win a man's heart easily than if you want to throw land-mines or grenades in his wallet."

"To go out to a nightclub whilst broke, and start sipping away slowly from a glass of whatever you are drinking, hop-ing that some gullible man will show up miraculously to buy you some drinks, is akin to a broke guy drinking some local opaque beer (i.e. chibuku) before going to a nightclub and then, after getting to the nightclub, sipping away majestically from the only bottle of 'imported' beer he's bought that night. Sooner or later, wa la byola (i.e. you will burp) in the middle of a conversation with a lady, or whilst dancing, and the notoriously smelly fumes of chibuku will betray the only bottle of beer you have bought, thus revealing your true identity."

"Do not be quick to question your friend's morals just because whenever you are with her most men are interest-ed in her, and not you. The problem could be with you, and not her."

"Those who are quick to volunteer neg-ative or bad information about their former boyfriend, fiancé or spouse are usually not better than the person they are condemning. Quite often, they are also a problem. I mean, how can you date a bad person, and even sleep with him, if he is that bad?

Someone cannot be bad just because you are no longer seeing him or her, or you can't have him or her. All along this is someone you had made the world to believe is the best thing to have ever happened to you until he or she was no longer a part of your life. You must be honest enough not to let bitterness, hate and sour grapes get in the way of objectivity. You could not have been sexually intimate with someone that you considered a bad person unless you are also a bad person."

"Where I come from in Africa, a man does not just impregnate another man's daughter and ask for forgiveness. The whole clan will be involved in the con-sultations. And he is expected to take up responsibility, unless he is a man of limited means."

"If you must settle disputes, it is best to use the court system or some recognized means of alternative dispute settlement, but not witchcraft. The problem with witchcraft, if at all it exists, is that it does not allow the other party to be heard. Judgments are almost always handed down by one litigant against his or her opponent through a peculiar process of judgment in default of appearance and without notice of hearing."

"If you are my friend and would like to bor-row some money from me, do not try to impress me by saying that you are just wait-ing for a cheque to clear or for some money that someone owes you. It will just upset me, especially that we both know that the purported cheque is non-existent. Be magnanimous enough to show humility that you are in need of help, otherwise I will ask you to go and wait for that cheque to clear."

"If we are having a good time as friends, and I am busy buying you beers, do not start tell-ing me stories about how someone owes you money, or how you are expecting a big cheque to clear soon. I did not ask for that information. Neither do I expect you to be telling me lies of how you are going to be in New York or London next month. I did not ask for such information. Just enjoy my beer quietly, and let us talk about sensible things."

"Growing up as a child in Africa, I re-member that the first thing that my father introduced me to, amongst the wealth and worth of his edifying posses-sions, was his library of books at our family home. Yes, he had a rich library at home, and he would ask me to read some of those books. At times, I thought that he was too harsh. But, I was young and naive. I now realize what a great father he was. He had a lot of foresight and wisdom. Some of it came not just because of his age, but more so because of having travelled widely back then and seen the world beyond the small 'myopic and parochial' world that I had been exposed to. It's only now that I understand these things in their right context."

"If you don't know how to engage or speak in public, or have a superficial understanding of the issues you are pretending to know, you will only last five to ten minutes of the one hour allocated to you for speaking before you begin to look blank, not knowing what to say next."

"In life, we all start out by quoting and citing other people's work. And there is nothing wrong with that. But there comes a time, as a scholar or public in-tellectual, when you have to ask yourself if it must continue like that or you must bring out your own original ideas that are worth putting out in the public domain. To achieve the latter, one ought to have matured intellectually. It is neither guesswork nor an art of chance. For, it is much easier for someone to copy and paste other people's ideas than to come up with his or her own original ideas. The latter requires creativity, innovation, clairvoyance, and critical and analytical thoughtfulness, as well as originality and insightfulness."

"Those that had more than enough yes-terday have often ended up swapping places in life with those that had nothing because they became complacent and neglected to pay attention to hard work. They believed instead in wrong and misguided critical factors of success. You cannot inherit, hijack or demand success. You must earn it."

"The thing about hard work is that you become your own man as you grow. You don't have to be known through some remote or obscure kind of association with some prominent name. When people ask that who is he or she, the generations to come will say that his or her works speak for themselves. And they won't waste time trying to locate or trace your famous relatives or associates. Your name alone, as established through your works, will be enough to tell the full story."

"To ask your father the name of the lady he was talking to suspiciously is tantamount to an act of treason. You must leave everything to God."

"If, for one reason or another, God for-bid, your father had a young girlfriend, there would be no point in getting upset. It won't change anything. Many cultures, especially in Africa, demand that you must treat that lady with respect whenever you see or meet her along the way. You cannot afford to disrespect her. Neither can you be contemptuous towards her. It would be dishonoring the unquestionable wisdom of your father. She is now your other 'mother', even though you may be older than her or may know something morally questionable about her character."

"To say that your father has gone out playing, or that 'Ba Daddy na ba ya muk-wangala,' when his friends are asking for him is against our African culture. Where I come from, even the most playful parent is never reported as having gone out playing because parents are taken to be serious people that have no time to waste. So, you simply have to say that the man is not around."

"In those cultures where children can go out playing, and are sometimes amiss or awol, without the parents knowing their whereabouts or what they are up to, God has had a bigger role to play in raising the children. As they say, 'Ala, ni Lesa fye...otherwise ku la kula fye kwati bana ba nsoka...'"

"The problem with some parents is that they are so obsessed with wishing that their children do better than other peo-ple's children. And when that does not happen, they become haters. We all have different talents. You cannot keep comparing your children to other people's children."

"If your imagination should run wild, let it not be on a weekend night or your payday when you are about to enter the sinful world, but on a day of worship when you are about to praise God like no man's business."

"In my native African culture, you don't say 'Shani boyi...' to someone who is not your peer. The white colonialists called almost all elderly African men as 'boy', signaling that the African man was not intellectually sophisticated enough to be called 'sir'. And so, the words 'Shani boyi...' especially when uttered by someone much younger, carry the same negative connotation to the African man. He does not want to hear that."

"Sometimes it is best to tell people what they want to hear. If you tell someone much younger than you that he or she is quite young, they may take offense if they consider themselves very accomplished or are prominent political appointees. And if you tell someone much older that he or she is too old they too may take strong exception to that. The best thing is to tell them what they want to hear to avoid problems."

"Many people tend to have some opin-ion already formed about what they expect to hear, and only ask to get a confirmation of their views. Anything to the contrary upsets them. Even someone asking for money does not expect you to say you do not have money."

"Do not look for a man's intention in his words...not even in his greeting. You may not find it there. Rather, you must look for it in his eyes."

"If you take off your clothes, you will see that you are just as human as any-body else. Don't let those clothes deceive you. We are all the same in God's eyes."

"You can't become a political critic just because you have been denied a political appointment as a cabinet minister. Only naive people will listen to you, especially that your anger is driven by your hunger."

"When the people vote and, for every single president that they vote for, they turnaround to say he is not good enough, you begin to wonder if the people themselves are good enough."

"No matter how pressed, two or more people cannot all sit on the toilet seat at the same time. Only one person is al-lowed at a time. And so it is with the presidency. There can only be one pres-ident in power at a time. The others have to wait until he or she is done."

"For the most part, politicians only see the wrongs of government when they are no longer in power. It makes you wonder. Is it that they only become wiser when they are no longer in power or what? Why don't they criticize government when they are in power? Is it that policies are only good when you are also eating, and they become bad when you are no longer eating or what? Surely, for some people to be deceived by those who only speak when they are hungry, and which folks often keep quiet as soon as they have something to eat, is a simple auction of democracy."

"No democracy is perfect. But in a political culture of tolerance where the opposition party can have enough air time on television to debate and discuss issues fiercely and freely, without any panga wielding cadres from the ruling party storming the television station to disrupt the debate, or the police declining to issue a permit for such gathering, there is what we call political civility and maturity. I waited all night to see panga wielding cadres from the ruling Democratic Party in America disrupt the Republicans' event, or the police arrest one of the leaders from the Republican Party, but none of that was forthcoming. Yet, the debate was fierce in criticizing the head of state on matters of domestic and foreign policy, with little or no degeneration into personalization of issues. And no teargas was ever fired by the police outside the arena to disrupt volatile crowds. People simply sat quietly and listened attentively. Everyone was well behaved. Now, that is what we call a debate."

"A man who is out on a first date with a fine lady cannot risk asking the lady if she is the one responsible for breaking the wind, or fouling the air, should the air suddenly become polluted. He should just swallow that air!"

"If you must break the wind, mighty or noxious, as it may be, at least have the decency and courtesy of excusing your-self, as opposed to making up a face like you don't know what's going on. After all, everyone, including divas, do fart. No need to feel shy."

"I have always admired something about corporate law, an area in which I specialize. You don't have to be emotional when dealing with corporate law. And you don't need activism or street protests to make your point. There are certain aspects of the law, especially those bordering on human rights or gender and development, where you can get away with just being spiritedly emotional, say, as an activist, even if the thought process is not well articulated."

"It's not only the lazy ones that look forward to the weekend. Even those that are broke somehow get excited as the weekend approaches. But, then, for what?"

"If two men should clash at a lady's home, with either of them waiting for the other to leave, the wiser is better served by taking off his shoes, and may be his shirt too, and then relaxing nicely while sprawled out on the bed or couch to signal to the other that he is going nowhere until the morning finds him there."

"Many a time when friendship is lost over a woman or a man, it is not always about breach of trust between friends, but about selfishness and greed. You cannot be possessive over something or someone that is not legally yours."

"In my life, I have learned a lot from people who have nothing. Sometimes, they don't have to say anything, but their unassuming smile and warmth in the midst of nothing simply disarms you. I have also learned a lot from the innocence of children. I cannot compare that experience with anything I have known in this pretentious world. The love in the eyes of a child is next only to God's love, free of all manner of corruption and sin. And I am still learning, and will continue to learn."

"Many a time I have prayed, 'Lord, don't let this night end...Let me dream on or let me experience whatever is there for me to experience.' And when I do lay me down to sleep, I know that I got no more heavy on my mind. I awake with the eagerness of love but to be met by the reality of a cruel world. Lord, have mercy on this world."

"Some thoughts cannot be captured in words fully. You must let the night speak for itself. Far and near, the heart will always be there. Sometimes tears of love flow not with a warning. And should love find you, do not stop the dance. Let the song play, and relax to the rhythm of the night. If love has a voice, then let it speak to your heart. You can't fight the feeling. I pray that God gives you the grace to love and to experience the power of love that you have so much longed for."

"If you must meet a nice man and get attracted to him, do not be reluctant or slow in disclosing your past, troubled, tumultuous or calm, as it may be. Soon-er or later, he might get around to the truth. So, you might as well say it."

"Do not wake up in the middle of the night, sweating and panicking, as you ask your girlfriend how many men she has slept with. Obviously, she will tell you that it's just one, or two at the most. What else do you expect to hear?"

"Do not go about bragging to your friends how your husband bought you this and that when those before whom you are bragging have no husband of their own. They may just know too much about your husband for you to take in."

"I can assure you, with a high degree of certainty, that the student in your class that was often obsessed with finding out what grade you got each time you all sat for an exam never went that far in his or her professional life. By contrast, those who excel and go far in life often don't behave that way."

"That your friend or neighbor has been de-nied a visa to go to America, France or England is no cause to celebrate. How does that make you any better than him or her when you are still in the same old place as you were yesterday? At least, he is trying."

"To go and visit a patient simply because you want to see or know how sick he or she is, or to go and visit someone in prison just because you want to see how miserable he looks, so that you can gossip about it, is not the way of a Christian. With such a mentality, your place is hell."

- Kenneth K. Mwenda

"Only failures rejoice or celebrate the failure or setback of others. Successful people don't rejoice or celebrate when other people encounter failure or set-back."

"If I come back with the truth, there will be nowhere to run to. It will be nothing, but the naked truth. So, it is best you come out clean now."

"There is always going to be someone somewhere who knows you very well even if you try to change towns or change your name. So, do not tell us lies. It's much safer and easier for you to tell us the truth than to face your past ghost when the truth emerges."

"For an irresponsible adult that is being kept by his aged parents in their home to pretend that he is looking after them is not only gross dishonesty but an ad-mission of hopelessness in the self."

"Do not panic or get upset when some-one asks you what your husband or wife does for a living, or whether or not he or she has been to school. Even those who are only dating, and are not mar-ried, face similar questions in various snobbish social gatherings. Be prepared to put your voice to the good of your partner, proclaiming lovingly that he or she takes care of you with a kind heart."

"People will always want to know, especially when they hear that you are faced with a predicament. Some already know, and will mind their own business. Others already know too, yet will want to make you feel bad by asking and pretending not to know. But if you were to excel and overcome the adversity they are talking about, they will not ask you or say anything because, in their small minds, they were expecting you to fail, and not to overcome the odds."

"If some good and decent people from overseas are interested in inviting your friend to a conference abroad, do not tell them that she has no passport. If they are looking for someone to hire for a vacancy in their organization or unit, do not tell them that there is nobody qualified out there to hire, or that you will get back to them with a name when you know very well that you do not in-tend to. If your boss were to ask you for an opinion on a colleague, do not be too quick to tell him or her all the negative things about the person. Your boss may just be assessing what you might say about him or her if someone else were to ask you the same question about the boss. You surely can find some good things to say about a colleague. And if they would rather give a chance to someone else, and not you, do not get upset and distance yourself from the whole process so that nobody else succeeds. In life, you cannot win like that."

"The law does not discriminate between a man that has smoked only one ball and a man that smokes habitually several balls. The punishment is the same. And so shall it be on judgment day. The punishment will be the same for various types of sinners."

"If you can't puff like the big boys, then don't smoke. You'll choke."

"When it comes to race relations and bigotry, many people are not comfortable to face the elephant in the room. We often choose to play safe by avoiding the topic. When it comes to tribalism and other ethnic divisions, we only speak out from a safe distance. But for how long can we keep pretending? For me to win your confidence or gain your acceptance, I don't have to wear a blonde wig or pick up a strange accent. Take me as I am, or nothing at all."

"The problem with an accent is that, no matter how polished or fine it may sound, it does not tell you much about the correctness of the underlying grammar or the depth of the analysis."

"If you are not careful, they will try to make you feel inadequate. They will question your abilities, your intellect, your competencies, and your very exist-ence. They will even want to know how you got where you are. Everywhere you go, that is the plight of the black man. Only God knows!"

"Do not invite me to the dance if you do not intend to ask me for a dance. I am not a statistic just for the sake of the number of invited guests. Rather, I want to be asked to dance as well because the difference between diversity and inclusion lies mainly in whether someone has been asked for a dance, or he or she was simply invited to the dance and then left alone."

"You cannot judge a man by the way he looks or walks. A man with red bloodshot eyes is not necessarily a drunkard or a smoker. Even the guy on the streets who has a thuggish walk is not necessarily a bad man or a thug. That bounce could be an inherited bounce in the family. Likewise, a lady with too much makeup on her face is not necessarily of questionable morals. But, why then are we quick to judge others? We must understand that some criminals are the most seemingly well-behaved and soft spoken people you will ever meet. Yet, they are criminals. And we easily warm up to such people forgetting that they could just be pretending or faking their demeanor. I am usually skeptical of a person that everyone says is such a nice person. And I will tell you why. A person cannot be nice all the time, everywhere and to everyone, unless he or she pretends or has no opinion of his or her own on any issue that could upset others."

"Even if there are no speed limits on the road to success, there can be break-downs or accidents along the way. It is wise to drive safely, and to be courteous towards other motorists or pedestrians, as you embark on your journey to success."

"Whatever is temporal and not permanent, wins you only temporal and not permanent respect. When it disappears, even the respect disappears. You just have to look at some former heads of state, former First Ladies, former ministers, and former corporate executives to see what I am talking about. Very few people will listen to them when they are no longer up there. And you would be lucky if people still greet you with the same enthusiasm and excitement as when you were up there. It is often best to invest in something that nobody can erase or take away from you."

"We all suffer from one form of addic-tion or another, though some people like to laugh at those that suffer from such addictions as alcohol or sex addic-tion. Alcohol addiction, as well as sex addiction, is commonplace in many people, though very few are willing to admit it. Other people are addicted to gossip. They just can't stop. Some are addicted to hate, hating on anyone that they fear will outshine them. Yet, there are also those that are addicted to religi-osity, constantly craving to be associated with the church or to be seen as holly, as well as those that are addicted to pursuing romance and love, constantly seeking to fulfill such dreams.

Some people are addicted to telling lies. Others are addicted to exuding arro-gance and pomposity. Yet, there are also those that are addicted to social media, food, music, or quarreling. The problem with addiction is that those that try to refrain from it often suffer from or experience withdrawal symptoms. They experience difficulties in letting go each time they try. And psychiatrists tell us that addiction is characterized by the inability to consistently abstain or refrain. It is a primary chronic disease of brain reward, motivation, memory and related circuitry. And so, we must show empa-thy towards one another as we all struggle with our respective addictions. I must confess that I am addicted to the pursuit of knowledge. It is a terrible ad-diction, with brilliant ideas constantly coming your way each time you try to rest from critical thinking. Even when my wife or my mother says, 'You have done enough work...you need to take it easy now...', the addiction of knowledge pursuit takes precedence. Addiction is a terrible thing. We all suffer from one form of addiction or another. Sometimes, although we may never admit it, we are just too proud to ask for help or to face reality."

- Kenneth K. Mwenda

"Those who ask questions often get themselves in trouble. Yet, the world can only develop if we do not stop ask-ing questions."

"Education often provides you with technical skills and a questioning mind, but not with loyalty. Make no mistake about that. But loyalty, as opposed to education or superior technical skills, can win you a place or promotion in the team. Many out there continue to sur-vive or thrive by not asking questions."

"Those who often try to play safe, walking on tiptoe to sneak in and peep at some latest on-goings pretty much stay unnoticed. And they remain that way in life – unnoticed! They only have themselves to blame. You cannot make a difference if you lack the character and courage to come out. Nobody won a medal by hiding."

"Some people worry a lot about how it could go wrong if they made a bold move or decision in life. But a wise man is more concerned about how it could go right and the great opportunities that that move can present, especially if the status quo is akin to that of a patient in a stable condition but not making much progress. To treat such a patient, it may be wise to change the type of treatment or medication. Staying put won't help."

"As long as you continue to do or say things for the sake of gaining public ac-ceptance, you will never be truly happy. The questions that you try to shy away from by being politically correct will never go away."

"A man is not free as long as he receives orders and commands from some superiors. He cannot say or do as he desires unless whatever he says or does is far from offending the superiors. And so, a man only becomes free when he begins to work for himself and to make his own decisions. Only then can he say or do as he pleases without worrying much about what the so-called 'superiors' think."

"It is how well you treat others that draws me to you. If, by contrast, you look down on others simply because of their race, tribe, lower station in life, humble car, small house, poor dressing, or lower educational levels, then I have a problem with you. I can assure you that you may not like me either."

"Don't ask me what car I drive, or the type of clothes or shoes that I wear. And don't ask me about how many mansions I own. Frankly speaking, I am passed that stage, and such things don't excite or move me. Rather, ask me about the fortress and fortitude of ideas that I have contributed and continue to contribute to society for the betterment of mankind."

"A lady that is quick to posit that she is married or engaged when some man asks her out to lunch or dinner is not answering the right question. The man is not interested in her marriage or en-gagement, and did not ask whether or not she is married or engaged. Besides, if you are married or engaged, does that mean you do not eat lunch or dinner? One must simply decline the invitation without adding extra talk time."

"Looking away and pretending not to have noticed when your friend is nicely dressed, or has something admirable that you so much crave for, but do not have, will not change an iota of a thing. You are better off offering your con-gratulatory message than pretending not to have noticed. Indeed, you can learn a thing or two from him or her that will help you to succeed or look good."

"If you were to ask a proud man where he studied, notwithstanding that he spent four (4) or more years of under-graduate studies in his native Third World Country before completing a short nine (9) months only taught Mas-ter's degree program, say, at Harvard University, the proud man is likely to mention only HARVARD, pontificating spiritedly, with bulging eyes, 'I went to Harvard', as if to intimidate you."

"A woman must understand why a man is presenting her with his business card when there is no business between them. By definition, a business card is for business, and not for women."

"A man holding out as a businessman who is quick to flash his business card, with no known office or business loca-tion, is often the first to suggest that he comes over to your office for a business deal. You will never hear him invite you to his office, save for a suggestion to meet up for drinks somewhere else in the social mix."

"The problem with wearing too much make-up is that, as the name 'make-up' suggests, you are probably making up for something you don't have; that is, looks! Now, you may choose to call make-up 'facials' or 'cosmetics' so that it sounds fancier. But even so, the word cosmetic entails something superficial, and not original. As an adjective, the word cosmetic involves or relates to treatment intended to restore or im-prove a person's appearance. And you don't want to be described that way be-cause your face does not require improvement or restoration."

"Pope Francis, despite being such a deeply spiritual and well-loved man in-ternationally, is not a prophet. He is simply the chief priest of the Catholic Church, considered as a successor to St. Peter. But, he is not a prophet. Neither is the great St. Pope John Paul II. Not even Nelson Mandela is a prophet. We must avoid the temptation of abusing and misusing grandiose religious titles such as prophet or prophetess just to soothe our own egos. Indeed, why are there so many so-called prophets and prophetesses in some of these Protestant churches today when great men such as those whose names I have highlighted above are not even close to being a prophet?"

"If a man were to tell you that he once or several times smoked marijuana in his youthful days, do not judge him by his past. Neither should you judge harshly a lady that would have sex for money. There are other people out there who have done worse off things and are now prominent men and women in society. But these men and women can't come out of the closet for fear of being judged harshly by society."

"If you were to ask various people ran-domly about what it is that gives them the greatest thrill of ecstasy in life, you would get very few honest answers. And those few honest answers would come not from the people that you think are honest, but rather from those that you probably consider crazy. Sometimes, it is crazy ones that are more honest and truthful than the sober and enlightened ones."

"A man full of big talk, empty promises and cajoleries, with no fixed abode, is like a dark cloud with no rain. You do not need an umbrella to face him."

"If your nephew at home, or the young houseboy, should bring to your house a young lady while you are at work, telling the lady that he is actually the owner of the house, and now tired of looking after you, the uncle, who does nothing but wake up in the morning to go to town for window-shopping, do not get upset. He means well but was just desperate. Understand this: he certainly has not changed the title deeds of the house. It's still your house. And so it is with life. Do not worry about those who try to profit from or take credit for your work. They are just desperate for some relief or recognition. But they can never take away your talent."

"If I sound like I hit hard with my mus-ings, please understand that I do not mean to provoke or injure people's feel-ings. Neither am I trying to crack the silent image in their mirror. Rather, I in-tend only to stimulate enlightened and erudite dialogue for the betterment of mankind. Such courageous effort re-quires calm temperament from all to allow the shared thoughts to distill peacefully."

"Change is often bitter and painful. But we can only change for the better if we can move out of our comfort zone to challenge and confront our fears. Oth-erwise, we remain stuck in the same old black hole of fear and uncertainty with no light at the end of the tunnel."

"The problem with human beings is that they only want to hear certain things, but not other things. It is those other things that I will talk to you about pointedly and assuredly. To appreciate what I have to say, you must be open-minded enough to move out of your comfort zone."

"It's important to laugh and smile. Laughter and humor, as psychologists tell us, are important for our good health. It is not every day that we must be seen to be serious as if we are pro-ducing a grand PhD thesis or discovering some new majestic theory. Even our Lord Jesus Christ, unlike the pretentious Pharisees, was cool with the apostles, sharing with them some great moments of wine and bread."

"People who don't joke, smile or laugh often look very ugly. Sometimes, their hearts can be ugly too. But when a not-so-good looking person is smiling or laughing, you can easily forget his or her looks by getting swayed into his or her warmth. And that warmth, and not his or her looks, will draw you in, whereas the cute or pretty looks of someone who is vain, cold or unpleasant will just smack of some repulsive attitude and unbearable arrogance."

"A woman who keeps warning and threatening her husband that one day she will walk out on him will never leave. Those who leave just leave with-out any habitual threats."

"In many developing countries, with rampant electricity power outages, or load-shedding, as the name goes, even a back-up generator is of not much use. Like a man troubled with premature ejaculation, the generator can only last for so long."

- Kenneth K. Mwenda

"Rampant electricity power outages, or load-shedding, as the name goes, are like a man troubled with erectile dysfunction. The disruption occurs just when you least expect it."

"Maybe when it comes to getting your dream job or your long-awaited promo-tion at work, or even securing your marriage or love affair, a talisman might work. I just don't know. But I can assure that talismans and other forms of superstition have no place or impact whatsoever when it comes to sitting for an examination in an institution of high-er learning."

"Where I come from in Africa, like in Asia or Latin America, we sometimes try to explain everything that perplexes us, including things that we do not understand fully, as the occurrence of the paranormal or a miracle. In cultures that are superstitious, almost everything is viewed from the prism of the supernatural or as part of the spiritual realm. For example, death or illness is not expected to occur without attributing it to someone who is busy maliciously and mysteriously disturbing the cosmic stratosphere. When a soccer player con-sistently scores from seemingly miraculous free-kicks we begin to ques-tion: how can it be? We are often looking at the spiritual realm for an-swers."

"The silent whispers of my heart are with you always. Even the psalms of Solomon speak of you. Who can deny that? Let the splendor of the Lord that radiates in you be a fountain of wisdom and love for those who care to love."

"If I could, I would have you right next to me now and forever. But I know that I only have to close my eyes, and you are with me...right next to me."

"Those who are afraid to love are afraid of opportunity, though love must not be equated with blind ambition. We must love with care."

- Kenneth K. Mwenda

"If you must love, you must love like an Arab man crossing the dessert. And if love should lead you to my corner, you must know that there is always a warm and safe place for you. We all have to learn to love a little more."

"In the western world, it is hard to keep up with notion of beauty. It is as if beauty is an evolving subject. Today, the focus can be on those that are slim and slender as the epitome of good looks. Tomorrow, everyone will be saluting those with an endowed posterior, with clothing companies beginning to make garments that reveal an endowed posterior supported by curvy handles. By contrast, in Africa, we have one standard that holds true for the most part."

"While a bonus has to be earned by those to whom it will be given, the African concept of 'mbasela', that is, some extras in addition to what one has paid for, should not be confused for a bonus. *Imbasela* is never earned and it calls for no hard work. It is simply the institutionalization of opportunism by the buyer. And so, *imbasela* has no justifiable place in a modern free market economy."

"It is impolite to ask a single mother who the father to her child or children is. She may take offense or it may remind her of a past she does not want to hear about. It is like asking a man why he is always broke."

"My many years of living abroad and traveling to so many different parts of the world has taught me something. When an African wants to borrow money, or is in need of financial assistance, he or she starts with a long winding story of explanations and justifications before finally making the request. The same is true for people from many other parts of the developing world.

By contrast, when an American or someone from Western Europe wants to borrow money, or is need of financial assistance, he or she will get straight to the point to avoid losing your attention. They often start with the request, and then move to some explanations or justifications, if any.

- *Kenneth K. Mwenda*

In comparison, for some people from Asia, especially the older generation, it is hard to figure out what they are trying to say when they want to borrow money or are in need of financial assistance. They tend to avoid the cultural shame and embarrassment of borrowing by using all manner of euphemisms and excessive politeness. You will miss the request if you are not culturally astute. You may think it is just a greeting."

"It is wise for people to stop bothering relatives, friends, colleagues or strangers that own expensive luxury cars to lend them their car for a wedding bridal party. Just walk or take a bicycle ride if you can't afford hiring a luxury car. Even the bride ought to be magnanimous enough to refuse being married off in a borrowed car."

"If the phone rings whilst you are in the toilet, it is best not to answer it instead of telling lies that you are in a meeting. Who are you meeting?"

"Where a married couple is sharing a room, nobody thinks of them suspiciously. We look at them with respect and honor. But where an unmarried couple is sharing a room, we imagine all manner of sin even though we are not witnesses to whatever is transpiring inside that room. Society is often quick to judge, and there is no right of appeal in a court of public opinion."

"You cannot hold someone hostage for the things that he or she uttered involuntarily at night whilst fast asleep. He is likely to have been out of his faculties. Words spoken or promises made under duress, or outside one's faculties, say, during a climax of coitus, or whilst asleep, are often not admissible in evidence."

"Human beings are strange. Your own young sister or brother could be a qualified medical doctor, yet you would rather listen to, or seek medical advice elsewhere from, say, a nurse or medical assistant not for privacy reasons but simply because you do not trust your own kind or just don't want to acknowledge him or her. Your own wife could be a lawyer, and a very good lawyer for that matter, yet you would rather listen to some young lawyers at the pub who, in turn, look up to your wife for inspiration. Why are we like that?

- *Kenneth K. Mwenda*

Human beings are strange. Some would rather promote glowingly on their Facebook wall books written by other people but not by their own friends or colleagues. We are constantly looking to the outside world for answers when answers are right there before us. We are constantly looking elsewhere for heroes when our true heroes are right there next to us. Why are we like that?"

"To borrow someone's car, without any form of payment being made akin to a car hire service, and then return it on almost empty tank, is not only disingenuous but a mark of true ungratefulness. Good manners and etiquette demand that if there was sufficient fuel in the car, you must return it just as you took it, or with higher levels of fuel, as a sign of gratitude and respect to the owner."

"Depending on how and where you were raised, if you see a black cat or hear the sounds of an owl at night, you are likely to react according to how you were raised or where you were raised, notwithstanding your high levels of education or your pretentious claims to aristocracy."

"To pretend that you do not need someone's help, and yet go behind that person in a crafty manner to try to get help from other people that you have known through, or because of, him or her, is not being clever or smart. It is equally disingenuous to send someone else to go and ask for help from that person, while pretending to be disinterested, so that you can benefit indirectly afterwards."

"Some people are too proud to get help from individuals who know them very well not because they don't need the help, but because of their own pride of not wanting to be seen to have been helped by others. You cannot grow and mature in life if you continue having difficulties accepting and acknowledging the help that you receive from others. We've all been helped at some point by others. And neither should it worry you when you hear that someone is saying that they helped you, unless you have a problem. A fact is a fact. It is not an opinion, hunch or speculation. It is a fact."

"It takes character to walk consciously in the other direction when everyone else is heading in one direction."

- *Kenneth K. Mwenda*

"There is a staircase that money cannot climb. It is wise to take that higher road. For, money cannot reach there, but you can if you will."

"The power and choice of words is something that a writer works with. Those are his tools. Rhetoric is built from that bench. But not even the best writer in town can express your love for someone the moment you fall deeply in love. Love just takes over like a tsunami."

"One who has experienced love has experienced happiness. For, happiness abides in love. And love is the fuel of genuine happiness. Where there is no love, there can be no genuine happiness. Indeed, there can be no love in material things but only a temporal euphoria steeped in utopia.

True happiness is an expression of love for our values and the things that we do, encounter, experience, share or achieve with a passion of self-fulfillment. But the love of money alone cannot lead to true happiness. For, money is just a means, and not an end. Sometimes, money simply brings you a new set of problems when you thought that you had arrived and are now set for life."

"It is a fundamental precept of legal ethics that lawyers generally should not behave like prostitutes, taking up each and every case that can bring them money even when they know that the case is a bad one with little or no chance of success. Perhaps, that is a notable difference between a legal practitioner and a legal scholar. The two edges of the chasm have different motivations."

"You must understand that, on a dinner date, it is not just the type of food or drink that you order that matters, but also how well-mannered you eat or drink the same as well as how classy the waiter chooses to describe the food or drink to you, together with your fine choice of mellow words befitting and complementing the waiter's description. If you must mildly smell the aroma of the red wine from a glass, holding the glass with much decorum and etiquette, before tasting a little of the wine to affirm the waiter's description, it is wise and prudent to do so. Your manners will determine how well the evening goes for the two of you."

- Kenneth K. Mwenda

"One who has travelled has more points of reference than one who has not. Traveling, like education or experience, is a source of knowledge. No matter how much you may try to study a people and their culture, you cannot understand them as much as one who has lived with them for some time. Neither is experience alone without education useful. You could have been doing whatever you are boasting of wrongly all these years. Education or experience alone, without much geographical and cultural exposure, is like an unpolished diamond that awaits to be cut and refined. You cannot affix such a diamond to a ring or earring until it has been cut and polished."

"Some people will tell you that they are writing a book. But you will never see that book. Yet, everywhere they go, they tell the same story. Others will tell you that they are about to get married. But you will never see them get married. Then, there are those who go about saying that they will soon commence some academic or professional studies. But you will never see them graduate. Yet, everywhere they go, they tell the same story."

"That a man has not told you that you are telling a lie does not mean that you are clever. Even if you try to play smart, your lies were known before you uttered them. Your character alone is enough to tell someone what you are capable of. Thus, the other person's silence is only meant to save you from further embarrassment."

"Those who tell a lie, like those who make false promises, have something in common. They are very quick at explaining themselves even when you have not asked them anything."

"If you must be efficient, do not prioritize those who do not take you for a priority. It is a waste of time. Rather, give your time and attention first to those who, as their priority, give you their time and attention. Some people have a problem. They end up spending their precious time trying to prioritize those who do not prioritize them."

- Kenneth K. Mwenda

"If I were to choose between launching a political party and launching a scholarly book, I would opt for the latter. No painful electoral defeat follows from launching a book."

"It is not easy to explain to someone that at your book launch you do not need a politician as the Guest of Honor because the honor is in the published work itself. If the book were to lack honor, then perhaps you could solicit for such honor. We have a tendency sometimes to think that we cannot do without clamoring to friendships and associations with those in positions of political power. We often want them to represent us at weddings and other social gatherings even when parliament has been dissolved constitutionally to allow for an election. Others even ask, 'Nga aba ku cha ume ninshi ba la ikala kwisa apa?' (English translation: 'And where will the groom's relatives sit?'), without realizing that such things have no room in a book launch."

"During an election, some people vote specifically to stop someone from being elected. That's all they are interested in. Others vote to empower and assist someone to be elected. It is like that in life. There are those who are just obsessed with stopping you from doing what you would like to do. Then, there are also those who are supportive because they would like to see you achieve your goals, or to see themselves gain eventually from your win."

"Waiting anxiously for election results is like constipation. It leaves you with anxiety. You just never know when it's gonna come out, or how big a win or loss it will be."

"More often than not, losing or winning an election has nothing to do with your capabilities. It simply reflects the mindset and thinking of the majority of those who voted."

"Not every disagreement or argument is anchored in sound reason. Many are devoid of logic. Others are jettisoned by untamed egos. But whatever it is, people can easily get along if they can just put aside their egos."

"Whatever you differ over, or motivates your differences, often defines your levels of thinking. You cannot afford to differ over petty or mediocre issues. Serious people disagree over gallant and noble ideas, and not triviality."

"I don't have to convince you, but at least I should be able to reason with you, unless you can't reason."

"If you would like to know how much a man is worth, do not look at his bank accounts or assets. Those are perishables. They don't last forever. And they don't tell the full story. Rather, look at his ideas. That is where the full story is. And that is where his greatest legacy lies."

"For me, there is nothing as fulfilling as the power of reason. We are all born with different talents. But if we are not able to reason soundly, we end up losing even the little that we are born with."

"In matters of sexual cleansing of widows, it is the close relatives of the deceased man that volunteer to cleanse the widow sexually, especially the nephews, brothers, or uncles that he used to look after or provide for financially, without realizing all along that they'd been lusting after his wife."

"As sad as it may seem, it should not come as a surprise that the law in some emerging economies does not expressly prohibit property-grabbing, including traditions of inheriting a widow of the deceased by his male relative. Although the practice of inheriting a widow is less common nowadays, in Zambia such practice is not proscribed or prohibited by law. A male relative of the deceased can therefore inherit the widow for himself. The law, albeit being legal, sometimes lacks legitimacy, especially when it comes to protecting the rights of some vulnerable members of society."

"A family member or relation who mourns with his eyes fixed on the assets of the deceased is up to no good, especially if he continues to wail the loudest, as he insults himself and throws all manner of proverbial profanity on himself in an effort to give the impression that he is the one who is more bereaved and affected than veryone else, surpassing even the hosts or 'owners' of the funeral."

"If a man of good standing in society were to confess that he used to smoke marijuana when he was young, or that he would often pick prostitutes in the prime of his youthful indulgence, many people will only remember that aspect of his life even though the man has done many greater things in life. So, people have now stopped confessing."

"A genuine man of God, like a good teacher or scholar, have something in common; that is, they both strive to pursue the truth to the fullest! And the truth can sometimes be very ugly."

"To claim that you are married, and insisting that people address you as 'Mrs' somebody, when in actual fact you are only someone's mistress or concubine, is a rather sad state of affairs that calls for a reexamination of your sense of self-worth. There is a clear difference between a home and a house in many African cultures, notwithstanding the big size of the physical building you live in."

"To tell lies that you'd qualified to go to your country's top university and that you even received an offer to that effect but chose to do something else with your life is something that many people that ended up in careers or professional training outside a proper university setting like to claim. The truth is that we may not be able to verify the validity of those claims, especially where a person appears to regret not having done a first degree back then, and is desperately trying to make up for the lost or missed opportunity. Anyone can claim anything. We are just not sure or convinced until we see the evidence."

"To remain quiet without disclosing to someone you are dating or are about to marry that you have a child born out of wedlock or from a previous marriage is not only dishonest, but rather unfortunate. Both men and women are morally obligated to make full and continuing disclosure about issues of paternity hidden deeply in the wardrobe. Not even your mother should shield you by claiming falsely to be the mother of your child so that you can get married quickly."

"It is morally unacceptable to terminate a pregnancy, especially where there is no risk to the life of either the mother or the child as well as where the pregnancy did not result from a forced or coerced attack. Every living being is entitled to life from the moment of conception, notwithstanding the philosophical arguments about when life actually begins. Those who choose, for one reason or another, to terminate a pregnancy cannot claim to be exercising a constitutional right to freedom of choice over another living being's life. Rather, they are committing murder. Life begins at conception, and not at birth. It is wise to own up before the true living God that you are a murderer."

"The truth is that some men and women are, for one reason or another, embarrassed or ashamed to be seen in public with their spouses. They would rather show up alone, with a lame excuse as to why their spouse could not join them. If you must marry, it is wise to marry someone you will not be hiding or leaving behind at home."

"The caliber of the man or lady that you date, or were dating, often sets the standard and tone of the type of folks that you are capable of dating. You can't suddenly claim to raise the bar if you have been dating low. Change takes time. It does not happen overnight."

"Marrying way up does not mean targeting rich or wealthy families to marry into. There could be a lot of illiteracy behind that wealth. Marrying way up simply means finding a well-enlightened and well-cultivated spouse who stands not on a pedestal of cheap arrogance or pride, but on his or her own pedigree of moral leadership, and profound intellect and wisdom."

"Many people that eventually turn out to be successful in whatever they are doing are those that are not resentful of successful people but rather are attracted to success and successful people. They end up learning from the best."

"To describe anyone who does better than you as, 'Ala yumfwa ulya' (English translation: 'S/he is very pompous, arrogant or too full of himself or herself'), when you have been trying to do the same but have not just been successful is a rather sad state of affairs. There is no difference between you and that person. It's just that you have been outdone or outclassed. Not everyone who has what you don't have can be said to be a brag. It is best to be honest and say, 'Na kumbwa' (English translation: 'I am envious'). That way, your heart will not be shouting profanity at you. Rather, it will motivate you to strive harder to get there too."

"The thing about public speaking is that you can, through perfecting your accent, using some rhetoric and big words, and such other flamboyant gestures, mesmerize those who do not have much training and knowledge on what you are talking about. But do not try that with those in the know. You will embarrass yourself. That's why politicians avoid going to present their ideas in such sacred places as the university, especially before an audience of faculty scholars, and not just undergraduate students."

"To keep insisting that people address you as 'Dr' somebody without disclosing where, or how, you got that title is like one who keeps bragging about the times when he or she lived in Europe or America without disclosing what he or she studied there, or went to do, and what qualifications or work experience he or she came back with. It is not enough that you went to, or lived in, America, France or England and have come back with a foreign accent. What were you doing there, and tell us what credentials or wealth you brought back with you?"

"If you don't know much about what others are discussing, try to speak slowly, with a deep and calm voice, as though you are thinking deeply, regurgitating most of the ideas of those that have spoken before you. Many will be convinced that you know a lot. And you can be the star at the meeting, until someone who knows you shows up to spoil the day!"

"Depending where you are in the world, not every dog that approaches you will run away with fear when you touch the ground as if to pick up a stone. In Africa, most dogs know exactly what that entails. In America or Europe, their dogs might interpret your gesture as trying to pick up a frisbee for the dog to play with. In short, the same mushroom that you would eat in Africa may be poisonous in China. You have to tread with caution. Not every fellow countryman or fellow African that you meet abroad may be nice to you. Every person is different. Sometimes, people from afar or a different ethnic background turn out to be more helpful."

"The horrors of your dreams at night are driven not only by your subconscious of the things that you experienced, encountered, saw or heard during the day, but also by the type of spouse, children, parents, pastors, neighbors, friends and relatives that you have around you. Thus, it is not unusual for your dreams at night to change or improve, depending on the neighborhood or home where you will spend the night. Dreams in some affluent neighborhoods are sometimes different from the dreams in some economically deprived or troubled neighborhoods. It all depends on the environment.

Some people would dream of someone trying to squeeze their neck to suffocate them at night while they were living in Africa. But the moment they left Africa, such nightmares ceased. Others would dream of their next-door neighbor making love to them. And that neighbor would be the first person to greet them in the morning, inquiring if they slept well. But it is possible that all these things could just be coincidences. Indeed, it could just be that someone is scared of facing the economic hardships he or she finds themselves in, and thus ends up with nightmares."

"For many aunties or grannies from the village, it matters that you not only get them individually the same type of gifts, but that the color of the gifts is also the same. Any slight color variation between the gifts, notwithstanding that the brand, style and everything else is the same is likely to lead to a furious protest, with one of them believing verily that you are biased and have favored the other. No matter how much you may to try to explain, it will still not call the protester out of her debilitating hunger strike. Neither will it end her rebellion and meal boycotts. The same is true for dependents in your household. To buy peace, you must get them the same color and type of clothes as your own children, especially if they are of a similar age and gender. Only a fellow African can understand. There are just certain aspects of our African culture and development that only the Africans themselves can understand best."

"The issue is not so much about how sexually suggestive a lady's mini-skirt or short dress is, but rather about how perverted your thoughts are. If you did not pay attention, you would not have noticed the suggestiveness. But you are busy paying attention. That's where the problem lies. You are the main culprit, and not her."

"If man can tame or delay his appetite for the three notorious W's that often slow him down, namely, wine, women, and worldly things, he is certainly guaranteed of going very far in life."

"Whether it is in a school exam, marital dispute, break-up of a relationship, or any other type of conflict or dispute, we can all achieve the same outcome without anyone getting hurt. The mentality of always wanting to see someone get hurt is a very primitive one. You don't have to fail students to prove to them that you are smarter. Rather, you examine students to get constructive feedback about the effectiveness of their learning. And you don't have to deny your spouse conjugal rights just to 'fix' him because he upset you. We can all achieve the same outcome without anyone getting hurt. We must not be tired of trying."

"Only when the zip of a boy's pants accidentally runs over the foreskin of his Johnny, almost circumcising him, does he realize the importance of taking it easy and paying attention to detail. Do not be in a hurry to get to the top without paying attention to detail. That zip of life might cause you excruciating pain if you are not looking carefully!"

"For many people, the problem with frolicking with stolen love is that it feels so good since it is not yours and you are just stealing it. But when you are caught, it can bring so much misery. As they say, the same thing that makes you happy gonna make you cry. But people don't listen, constantly driving themselves to the edge of madness."

"No matter how poor or desperate you are, it is unwise to buy and wear secondhand underwear. One is better off going without any if you cannot afford a new pair. After all, a cool breeze shall follow your imprisoned articles to set them free once you let go. Do not accept to play second fiddle."

"Election time is a prophetic moment for opportunistic lawyers to make money. Many lawyers prepare election petitions a year ahead of time, lying low and just waiting to ambush potential clients that have lost an election. It's business as usual, with little to do with justice."

"When they see you talking to a lady, some people have a tendency to reach a conclusion quickly. Thereafter, they try to walk backwards to see who it is that they think you are dating or where it all started from, if anything. Look, you cannot arrest someone and then start working backwards to trump up charges against him. It should be the other way; that is, you have to have charges before you can arrest, and not mwa ikata umuntu elo mwa tampa uku tontokanya (English translation: 'You arrest someone and then you start to think of a crime to charge him with'). It is very poor reasoning and logic to start with a conclusion, and then work backwards to find a suitable methodology to validate the conclusion. That's not science. I don't even know what to call it. But many people still reason like that. They start with a conclusion, and then work backwards to a methodology."

"That in your entire life you have never heard your father tell your mother that 'I love you' does not mean that you cannot tell your wife that 'I love you.' What are you afraid of? Who else will tell her those words if you don't? It is a misnomer to think that the words 'I love you' are meant for young people who are still not married, or by a man running after a young lady. 'I love you' is not a password to access a system such that the moment you're granted access you don't need to re-enter the password!"

"To understand romance as simply being an art of physique in the bedroom is where many people get it wrong. It does not have to be a fight always. Sometimes, just holding hands and saying the right words softly in the moonlight and on a quiet evening can make a difference. At times, your choice of quality music and fine drink, as well as your dressing and perfumed scent, in addition to your assurance of safety and patience, can help to claim the night."

"A romantic life is not always about money. Rather, it starts with creativity and the right touch of finesse. You can do a lot with very little. You can have all the money in this world, drive the fanciest car, or live in a mansion, but if you don't know how to press the right buttons or how to conduct yourself through an intelligent conversation, with good and fine manners, you ain't going nowhere. The taste of a

- Kenneth K. Mwenda

fine wine starts with how the waiter describes the wine to you and how he pours it into the glass before you hold the glass in the right manner and anoint the wine with a few inspiring words at tasting."

"To show up or hear from you only when you have a problem is not friendship, but exploitation."

"Where I come from in Africa, because of superstition, some people try to hide information about the successful things that their children or close family member are doing at home or abroad. But they are quick to talk about other people's children. We live in a strange world. You can have a friend in Africa writing to you in the diaspora daily, and even communicating with you over the phone, without ever disclosing that his own brother or sister lives right next to where you are.

Others are just ashamed to say anything if their close family members are not doing well. Yet, it should not be like that. Then there also those who like to exaggerate and embellish the modest accomplishments of their close family members at home or abroad. We live in a strange world."

"Men must understand that a female friend who tries to be defensive of her own well-being, or even gets upsets, when you, as a married man, are singing great praises about your wife is a threat to humanity and must be avoided at all costs."

"Sometimes the respect that you accord a person who has been there for you is deep enough a statement of gratitude. You can say many 'thank you' words over and over again, but if you are not respectful and courteous to that person, your words don't mean much at the end of the day."

"When two people love each other, but, for one reason or another, just can't have each other, either one of them or both will eventually not stand the other, unless they are both very mature about it. You must understand where the energy of anger, irritability and indignation often comes from."

"Sometimes, you don't have to look behind you to see who is watching or following you. You can simply feel their eyes on your body. The radiant heat of their curious eyes is enough. Those eyes can undress you or even abuse you."

"If you would like to know how much a man is worth, do not look at his bank accounts or assets. Those are perishables. They don't last forever. And they don't tell the full story. Rather, look at his ideas. That is where the full story is. And that is his greatest legacy."

2

CASE STUDIES

I TOLD HIM THAT HE COULD
KEEP HIS MONEY

This evening, as I was picking up some groceries from some local shop, I was taken aback when the cashier told me that the till or register was not working. By then, I had already presented him with three one hundred dollar bills ($300). So, he owed me some change to the amount of approximately $60.

With the till down, he proceeded to get some loose change from the groin region of his underwear, claiming that he kept the money there to safeguard

- Kenneth K. Mwenda

it from thieves. I said to myself, "No way!" I declined to accept or touch the visibly dump notes from his underwear! I was so upset that he could think that I would get the money coming from his underwear. What a jerk! So, I just drove off without getting my change.

WHEN THIEVES ORDER
EVERYONE ON THE BUS TO UNDRESS

It was in the early 1980s on a long distance bus from Ndola to Mufulira, two major cities on the Copperbelt Province of Zambia. The bus route was notoriously famous for criminal attacks on motorists by bandits and thugs that would cross into Zambia from the neighboring country of Zaire, now known as the Democratic Republic of Congo (DRC).

Pretending to be police officers, and wearing police uniform, a gang of criminals stopped a commuter bus at a purported check-point. It was only when the bus had stopped that the driver and the passengers realized that the men in uniform were not cops but a bunch of bandits. The men were armed with military assault weapons, and they ordered everyone on the bus to strip completely naked. It was a terrible ordeal.

One of my male cousins was traveling on that bus in the company of his mother-in-law and father-in-law. And all the passengers were ordered to stand in a queue while naked before being allowed (in their naked state) to board the bus again. And they all had to leave behind the clothes they were wearing as well as their luggage before the criminals could release the bus without harming anyone. All the passengers had no choice but to comply. It was a terrible sight, a bus full of naked adults and children heading straight to the police station with a naked driver at the stirring wheel.

Some people tried to cover their private parts with their bare hands, but even so their behinds remained exposed. My cousin told me that he could not look at his in-laws throughout the rest of the journey. Neither could they, at least, so they claimed!

Children were traumatized after seeing the funny ungodly-looking body structures and fea-tures of some naked adults. A number of men and women who tried to cover and conceal their private areas with their hands could hardly maintain that concealment as they had to use their hands also to wipe off tears from their eyes. It was a terrible sight.

The bus arrived in Mufulira full of naked men and women, all seemingly looking away from each other, although stealing occasional glances wherever and whenever a chance pre-sented itself. My cousin narrated how for the first time he saw a man with some kinky Afro hair in the wrong places that had grown into small dreadlocks. Apparently, the man got detained by the police for being a danger to public safety with his annoying dreadlocks! Thankfully, those days are long gone now! Never again...

THE DAY I STOPPED LISTENING TO RADIO COMMENTARIES OF LIVE SOCCER GAMES

It was a bright Sunday afternoon in the mid-1990s, and Zambia was playing against Zimbabwe at the famous Rufaro Stadium in Harare, Zimbabwe. I was visiting Zambia on vacation from England. In the morning, I had gone to church for Sunday worship. So, I was feeling very spiritual and all, trying my best to stay that way until a friend of mine came to pick me up so that we could watch the televised soccer game together at his place over a beer or two.

Shortly after the game kicked off, there was some interruption in the live TV trans-mission of the game, leaving us with no option but to turn to the radio. The Zambian soccer authorities had arranged for both English and Nyanja/Ngoni commentaries of the game. Because we wanted to be seen to be more patriotic to our country, both my friend and I opted to listen to the Nyanja/Ngoni commentaries. The game was tight. At some point, one Zambian soccer legend, Kalusha Bwalya, got the ball, and then skillfully dribbled past three players in succession. And the Nyanja/Ngoni soccer commentator went wild with excitement, announcing on radio:

"Uyo Kalusha, anyenga umozi, anyenga na wina,

ango nyenga tyala, na wina, ango nyenga... Uyo, ni mwa muna...!"

I could not believe what I heard. Now it is a bit hard for me to translate into English or my native language, Bemba, what those exact words would have meant. However, a mild and modest translation points to profanity of a man taking to bed one woman after another. I looked at my friend if at all he had also heard the Nyanja/Ngoni commentaries on the radio. At that point, my friend's young son walked in with some snacks for us. He brought us a cup of coffee each with some French toast. My friend is Luvale from Northwestern Province in Zambia. And when he asked his son, while not paying much attention, what the boy had brought us on the coffee tray, the boy responded in the Luvale language: "Mbolo!"

Now, that just worsened the situation for me because the word mbolo in my native lan-guage means 'manhood' or the 'person' of a man. Yet, in Luvale it means 'bread'! I politely excused myself from the coffee, fearing to partake in mbolo with coffee.

- Kenneth K. Mwenda

IS MASTURBATION A SIN?

We cannot run away from such seemingly taboo or highly sensitive topics when, in actual fact, they do affect a good many of the so-called religious people. To argue that the word 'masturbation' is not found or mentioned anywhere in the Bible, and that therefore the act of masturbation is not a sin, is nothing but the pursuit of a red herring.

Even an unmarried Christian guy who claims that he only kisses his so-called 'church-sister', and does nothing more is guilty of fornication the moment his mind begins to entertain remotely some lustful thoughts. The mind has its own ways! The Bible tells us clearly that a man who looks at a woman lustfully that is not his wife, whether the man is a prophet, bishop, senior pastor or priest, has committed adultery. And so it is with fornication. The evil thought alone is enough.

Now, I have read some interesting posts from a number of church leaders in the Pentecostal Christian movement on the issue of whether or not masturbation is a sin. But I have not read anywhere from any psychologist or medical doctor that someone can masturbate successfully without entertaining some sexual thoughts, notwithstanding that the masturbator was actively masturbating with such fury to bring about the desired result quickly. Yet, these are some of the tough questions that we all want to shy away from. But there is no running away. It is time for some tough conversation.

Some Pentecostal pastors say that masturba-tion is a sin. Others say it is not. At the outset, I must state that I am neither a pastor, bishop, prophet nor a saint. Rather, I am a legal philosopher. From that perspective, I can enter the forests to look for some intellectual firewood. The philosophical premise here is to try and understand the salient aspects of the epistemology underlying the morality of masturbation. Is it morally wrong or right for a Christian to masturbate? And, is it a sin for a Christian to masturbate?

Closely related to these questions are issues such as the probable sinfulness of oral sex (not just kissing, but blow-job) and anal sex within the institution of marriage. Here, I have deliberately avoided the issues of oral and anal sex outside marriage because it is well and nigh settled by the court of public opinion that adultery and fornication are sins.

Likewise, is it morally wrong or right for a married Christian couple to use condoms when asserting their conjugal rights, or does the use of condoms militate against the Christian notion of holy sex in marriage? Further, we could ask: Is it morally right for married Christian couples to use condoms as a means of family planning, or should they rely solely on such natural methods of family planning as counting days or the often pitifully faulty 'withdrawal method'? These are some of the tough questions that we all want to shy away from. But there is no running away. Let the discussion begin.

IS MARRIAGE SO ESSENTIAL FOR COUPLES, OR SHOULD THEY SIMPLY CO-HABIT AND PROCREATE FREELY OUTSIDE OF THE INSTITUTION OF MARRIAGE?

The question presented above was under discussion on a US radio station recently, as I was driving to work. A female correspondent wrote to the radio show host, explaining that she has an ongoing fantastic relationship with her longtime boyfriend. The two broke up, but are now back together. And they have been co-habiting for some time now, with two children between them. Although most of the lady's friends and relatives have been telling her to formalize the relationship and get married to the man, she disagrees and says that she sees no reason why the two should get married when more than seventy percent (70%) of married people, according to her, are miserable. The lady makes a strong claim that she and her boyfriend get on just fine, and that getting married won't change a thing.

The radio show host provided a contrasting view by stating that marriage is the real deal, in accordance with God's plan, and that human beings should not try to alter or adjust God's decree for their own self-serving interests. He went on to add that a good marriage enhances the quality of life of the couple and the family. And he was quick to point out also that where someone makes a miserable choice or decision about marriage, then their marriage will enhance that miserableness. Accordingly, marriage, as argued by the radio show host, is an enhancer of whatever good or ugly situation you get yourself into.

Now, in the age of modern science and tech-nology where procreation (i.e. having children) can be achieved through means such as artificial insemination, relying on an anonymous sperm donor, or where individuals can effectuate and achieve sexual pleasure through the use of sex toys, some commentators are beginning to question the relevance of marriage.

Closely related to this issue is the whole argu-ment of human rights. In many modern democracies, individuals have been championing liberties that they believe are not to be proscribed by any societal norms or standards of human sexual morality. Are such claims predicated on human rights or human wrongs? If they are about human wrongs, how can we right these wrongs? Indeed, what is the essence and meaning of marriage? Is it a union between a man and a woman or between people of the same sex or gender? And what is the moral or ethical justification for a woman to choose on her own to have a child out of wedlock, denying that child the right to have a father-figure when the child is born? Should individuals be making such self-serving and selfish choices on behalf of the unborn? Or, do the unborn also deserve a family with a father-figure?

By parity of reasoning, can we justify abortion in the absence of certain extenuating circum-stances under the law? Can a woman decide on her own to deny the unborn child the right to life? Shouldn't the interests and rights to life of the child also matter? At what stage in the preg-nancy can a child be said to have entitlements to life?

THE CHALLENGES OF A BEMBA-SPEAKING MAN DISCUSSING POLITICS AND ECONOMICS

Although I do not blog about the politics of my native country, Zambia, it is becoming increasingly difficult for me to discuss offline certain economic and political fundamentals with some of my relatives who originated from the Luba-Lunda Empire. Recently, an American friend of mine joined me for dinner, together with two Zambian friends, Katebe Chungu and Bwalya Mwila.

My American friend explored various aspects of the Zambian economy and politics at the dinner table, probing about domestic and foreign policy issues. I gave my responses cautiously, without selling out on the dignity of my country and people. I then turned to Katebe for his input on the current economic environment back home in Zambia. Instead of explaining the underlying economic fundamentals, which he clearly did not understand, Katebe goes:

"Ba Yama (uncle), when I think of the econo-my back home and what those guys are doing, ine ku mutima kwa fita (i.e. my intuition tells me things are not looking good)."

But we were not discussing intuition here! Ra-ther,

we were discussing economic policies. It's quite hard to reconcile gut feelings or intuition with proper analysis.

And when Bwalya's turn to comment on the economy came, he looked at me, while holding a big chunk of roasted meat to his mouth, and said:

"Ba Yama (uncle), na mu landa fyonse kale. Nifyo fine, mukwai. Nga kuti na sosa shani? (i.e. You have said it well. What more is there to add?)"

At that point, I realized the challenges faced by my two brothers, Bwalya and Katebe. I tactfully took over the conversation and was left to chat with my American friend the whole evening because Katebe ena ku mutima kwa li fita, supposedly due to something unknown about the Zambian economy, while Bwalya believed that I had said everything that he was going to say, that is, if at all he was even going to say anything.

CONTENDING AFRO-CENTRIC TRADITIONS IN THE DIASPORA

One particular Saturday in early January 2016, as we were having family breakfast, my son shared with me that one of his teeth that was almost falling off had finally come out. Being an African father, as I am, I told my son to keep the tooth properly so that I could perform a traditional African ritual the following day early at dawn. And here is how the ritual is performed.

A young person whose tooth has fallen off hands over the tooth to a family elder at dawn. And the responsible elder comes out of the house, almost half-naked, holding the tooth in the hand while facing the rising sun, and throws the tooth far in the direction of the rising sun. He then utters some incantation. In my culture, you do not just throw away a broken tooth anyhow, so we were told by the elders.

And so, as I was getting ready to leave the house at 05:00 a.m to face the rising sun, my son alerted my wife to come and see what was happening. My son was worried because at school the teacher told his class about a lovely tooth-fairy who comes along to bring you a nice gift when your tooth falls off. But where I grew up in Africa, there were no such things as a tooth-fairy. Like many in my age group, the concept of a tooth-fairy continues to be alien. We would simply throw a broken tooth to the rising sun. That's what we grew up with.

But my wife would have none of that, citing scientific theories from her medical profession that such rituals are just mere superstition, and that I could get arrested if my neighbors saw me performing that primitive ritual in an affluent American neighborhood! I tried to explain the importance of keeping our African traditions, but she countered that traditions only make sense where they are backed up with scientific evidence or logic. I tried to explain to her that where we come from in Africa, like in many other parts of the developing world, we do not always follow logic. Sometimes, things just happen. And that's just how it is.

Hitherto, my wife and I are still debating this issue. But I am convinced about the need for me to come out of the house at dawn, almost half-naked, to face the rising sun with a tooth in my hand! After all, aren't there some things around us that are incapable of explanation, including strange claims of UFO or alien sightings in America?

ABOUT THE AUTHOR

Prof. Kenneth K. Mwenda
PhD, LLD, DSc(Econ)

http://www.kennethmwenda.com

A distinguished thought leader and public intellectual, **Prof. Kenneth K. Mwenda** read law at Oxford as a Rhodes Scholar. He has also taught law at top universities in the United States of America (US), the United Kingdom (UK) and South Africa. A Fellow of the British Royal Society of Arts (FRSA), Prof Mwenda is a recipient of several international academic awards, including a competitive fellowship from Yale University Law School in the US. Most recently, he gave the 2015 Distinguished Lecture at the University of Nairobi Law School in Kenya, and was appointed as Extraordinary Professor of Law in the Faculty of Law at the University of Pretoria, South Africa. He has also held previously the position of Extraordinary Professor of Law at the Centre for Human Rights, the University of Pretoria. Based in Washington DC, Prof. Mwenda is the Program Manager and Executive Head of the World Bank's Voice Secondment Program, a major capacity-building initiative of the Board of Executive Directors of the World Bank.

Prof. Mwenda has had a stellar academic career as well as an outstanding professional life a leading international development practitioner, travelling to more than thirty countries worldwide. His is a fine blend of theory and practice, with many years of international experience in both academia and international development. Prof Mwenda has maintained a parallel academic and professional life, publishing academic books and other scholarly work in top journals and law reviews as well as holding various senior academic appointments at leading universities internationally, while serving with the World Bank. A member of the editorial boards of several scholarly journals, including the *Journal of*

International Banking Regulation and the *Africa Finance Journal,* he is also an occasional editor of the *Journal of African Business,* and was until recently the joint Editor-in-Chief of the World Bank's *Law, Justice and Development Book Series.*

With sustained thought leadership in academia, in addition to valuable experience in international development practice, Prof Mwenda is a widely recognized authority in his field of expertise as well as a highly sought-after speaker that has been interviewed and quoted by numerous print and broadcast media, including the *New York Times* (US), the *Voice of America* (VOA, US), *CCTV* (US), the *Times* (UK), the *British Broadcasting Corporation* (BBC, UK), and *Sky TV* (UK). In 2008, after a rigorous and thorough examination of Prof Mwenda's selected scholarly books and peer-refereed journal articles by a distinguished panel of top international legal scholars, Prof Mwenda was admitted by Rhodes University, a leading university in South Africa, to the rarely awarded Higher Doctorate degree of Doctor of Laws (LLD). It was the first time ever in the rich academic history of that university that such an award was being conferred in the Faculty of Law! Six years later, in 2014, after another rigorous and thorough examination of Prof Mwenda's other substantial portfolio of scholarly books and peer-refereed journal articles by a distinguished panel of eminent international scholars, Prof Mwenda was admitted by the University of Hull, a leading British university, to the rarely awarded Higher Doctorate degree of Doctor of Science in Economics (DSc(Econ)). It is

162

important to stress that in the entire English speaking world, Prof. Mwenda is arguably the only senior legal scholar to have earned two Higher Doctorate degrees in two different disciplines! Higher Doctorates, it should be emphasized, are never the immediate step after a PhD. Rather, they are reserved for those internationally recognized senior scholars that have made exceedingly significant contributions to a science or body of knowledge through exceptionally insightful and distinctive scholarly publications, earning them recognition as international authorities in the field of research that forms the basis of the degree.

Further, Prof. Mwenda holds a PhD in Law from a leading British university, the University of Warwick. At the World Bank, he has served additionally as Senior Legal Counsel in the Legal Vice-Presidency as well as Senior Legal Counsel in the World Bank's Integrity Vice-Presidency. All in all, Prof. Mwenda has written more than twenty-five (25) scholarly books and over ninety (90) articles in leading law reviews and academic journals. Prior to joining the World Bank, he served as an Assistant Professor of Law at the Faculty of Law, the University of Warwick, in the UK. Prof Mwenda has also taught as Adjunct Professor of Law at American University Washington College of Law (WCL) in Washington DC. His scholarly work is cited frequently as authority not only in academia, but also by the courts of law, most recently by the Supreme Court for the Republic of Zambia in the case of *Ventriglia and Ventriglia v. Eastern and Southern Africa Trade and Development Bank and*

163

Robert Simeza SCZ NO. 13 OF 2010 (Appeal No. 11/ 2009). His other scholarly work has been seminal in some of the research work and country assessments carried out by the International Monetary Fund (IMF), the World Bank, the Asian Development Bank (ADB) and the Inter-American Development Bank (IADB).

In addition, Prof. Mwenda holds, *inter alia*, the prestigious BCL degree from the University of Oxford (UK) and an MBA degree from the University of Hull (UK), with subsequent executive leadership training from Cornell and Georgetown Universities, respectively. His first professional law degree, a Bachelor of Laws (LLB), is from the University of Zambia where he graduated in 1990 in the top one percent (1%) of his class. He was admitted to the Bar in Zambia in 1991, as the best Bar admission student. Prof. Mwenda is a US Certified Anti-Money Laundering Specialist (CAMS) as well as a Fellow of the British International Compliance Association (FICA). He has served as Visiting Full Professor of Law at a number of leading universities in Europe and South Africa, including the University of Miskolc in Hungary, the University of Cape Town (UCT), the University of Western Cape (UWC) and the University of Zambia. He has also given many lead lectures and presentations at major US universities, including George Washington University, the University of Maryland, Duke University, Temple University, and the University of South Florida.

OTHER BOOKS BY THIS AUTHOR

2016

Kenneth K. Mwenda, **Anthology in Law and the Social Sciences**, Vol. 2, (Toronto, Canada: Africa in Canada Press, 2016).

2016

Kenneth K. Mwenda, **Anthology in Law and the Social Sciences**, Vol. 1, (Toronto, Canada: Africa in Canada Press, 2016).

2016

Kenneth K. Mwenda, **Public Intellectualism and Socio-Political Inquiry through Metaphor and Musing**, Vol. 4, (Toronto, Canada: Africa in Canada Press, 2016).

2016

Kenneth K. Mwenda, **Public Intellectualism and Socio-Political Inquiry through Metaphor and Musing**, Vol. 3, (Toronto, Canada: Africa in Canada Press, 2016).

2016

Kenneth K. Mwenda, **Public Intellectualism and Socio-Political Inquiry through Metaphor and Musing**, Vol. 2, (Toronto, Canada: Africa in Canada Press, 2016).

2015

Kenneth K. Mwenda, **Understanding
Securities Law and Regulation in Zambia**,
(Cape Town, South Africa: Juta Academic
Publishers, 2015).

2015

Kenneth K. Mwenda, **Public Intellectualism
and Socio-Political Inquiry through
Metaphor and Musing**, Vol. 1, (Toronto,
Canada: Africa in Canada Press, 2015).

2011

Kenneth K. Mwenda, **Public International
Law and the Regulation of Diplomatic
Immunity in the Fight against
Corruption**, (Pretoria, South Africa: Pretoria
University Law Press (PULP), 2011).

2011

Kenneth K. Mwenda, **Contemporary Issues
in Zambian and English Company Law: A
Comparative Study**, (Amherst, NY: Teneo
Press, 2011).

2010

Kenneth K. Mwenda, **Legal Aspects of
Banking Regulation: Common Law
Perspectives from Zambia**, (Pretoria, South
Africa: Pretoria University Law Press (PULP),
2010).

2010

Kenneth K. Mwenda, W. Fischer, H. A. Amankwah and D. Goulding, **German Hyperinflation 1922/1923 – A Law and Economics Approach**, (Cologne, Germany: Josef Eul Verlag, 2010).

2009

Kenneth K. Mwenda and G.N. Muuka (eds), **The Challenge of Change in Africa's Higher Education in the 21st Century**, (Amherst, NY: Cambria Press, 2009).

2007

Kenneth K. Mwenda, **Comparing American and British Legal Education Systems: Lessons for Commonwealth African Law Schools**, (Amherst, NY: Cambria Press, 2007).

2007

Kenneth K. Mwenda and W. Fischer (eds), **Country of Origin – A Law and Economics Approach to the Concept of 'Made in Australia'**, (Cologne, Germany: Josef Eul Verlag, 2007).

2007

Kenneth K. Mwenda, **Legal Aspects of Combating Corruption: the Case of Zambia**, (Amherst, NY: Cambria Press, 2007).

2006

Kenneth K. Mwenda, **Legal Aspects of Financial Services Regulation and the Concept of a Unified Regulator**, (Washington DC: The World Bank, 2006).

2006

Kenneth K. Mwenda, **Combating Financial Crime: Legal, Regulatory and Institutional Frameworks**, (Lewiston, NY: The Edwin Mellen Press, 2006).

2006

Kenneth K. Mwenda, **The Legal Administration of Financial Services in Common Law Jurisdictions: with special attention to the dual regulation system in Zambia**, (Lewiston, NY: The Edwin Mellen Press, 2006).

2006

Kenneth K. Mwenda and V. Mosoti (eds), **Contemporary Issues in International Economic Law**, (Cologne, Germany: Josef Eul Verlag, 2006).

2006

H. Kyambalesa and M.C. Houngnikpo; with contributions from Kenneth K. Mwenda and G.N. Muuka, **Economic Integration and Development in Africa**, (Aldershot, UK: Ashgate Publishing Co., 2006).

2005

Kenneth K. Mwenda, **Anti-Money Laundering Law and Practice: Lessons from Zambia**, (Lusaka, Zambia: University of Zambia (UNZA) Press, 2005).

2003

Kenneth K. Mwenda, and D.A. Ailola, (eds), **Frontiers of Legal Knowledge: Business and Economic Law in Context**, (Durham, NC: Carolina Academic Press, 2003).

2003

Kenneth K. Mwenda, **Principles of Arbitration Law**, (Parkland, FL: Brown Walker Press, 2003).

2002

Kenneth K. Mwenda (ed), **Banking and Micro-finance Regulation and Supervision: Lessons from Zambia**, (Parkland, FL: Brown Walker Press, 2002).

2001

Kenneth K. Mwenda, **Zambia's Stock Exchange and Privatisation Programme: Corporate Finance Law in Emerging Markets**, (Lewiston, NY: The Edwin Mellen Press, 2001).

2000

> Kenneth K. Mwenda, **Banking Supervision and Systemic Bank Restructuring: An International and Comparative Legal Perspective**, (London, UK: Routledge-Cavendish Publishing, 2000).

2000

> Kenneth K. Mwenda, **The Dynamics of Market Integration: African Stock Exchanges in the New Millennium**, (Parkland, FL: Brown Walker Press, 2000).

2000

> Kenneth K. Mwenda, **Contemporary Issues in Corporate Finance and Investment Law**, (Washington DC: Penn Press, 2000).

1999

> Kenneth K. Mwenda, **Legal Aspects of Corporate Capital and Finance**, (Washington DC: Penn Press, 1999).

Thank you!

FOR YOUR READERSHIP

INDEX

FEEDBACK

> **Now that you have read the book ...**

Was it interesting?

Did you enjoy what you wanted to read?
Was there any room for improvement?

Let us know at:

http://www.kennethmwenda.com/feedback

Your feedback is highly appreciated.
Thank you!

- Kenneth K. Mwenda

Would you like to buy a copy of

PUBLIC INTELLECTUALISM
AND
SOCIOPOLITICAL INQUIRY
THROUGH METAPHOR AND MUSING

by Kenneth Mwenda?

Order Online!

Please visit:
http://www.kennethmwenda.com/books

www.ingramcontent.com/pod-product-compliance
Lightning Source LLC
Chambersburg PA
CBHW071909220626
47052CB00002B/273